TREE-HUGGING CATS

First Published in Great Britain 2024 by Mirador Publishing 2

Copyright © 2024 by Julian Worker

All rights reserved. No part of this publication may be reproduced or transmitted, in any form or by any means, without permission of the publishers or author. Excepting brief quotes used in reviews.

First edition: 2024

Any reference to real names and places are purely fictional and are constructs of the author. Any offence the references produce is unintentional and in no way reflects the reality of any locations or people involved.

ISBN: 978-1-917411-16-5

Tree-Hugging Cats

Julian Worker

Also by the author

Tomcat Tompkins
Sports the Olympics Forgot
Travel Tales from Exotic Places
Julian's Journeys
40 Humourous British Traditions
Diary of a Buddhist Cat
Our Cats in Amsterdam

The Inspector Knowles Mysteries
The Goat Parva Murders
The Manton Rempville Murders
The Frisby Waterless Murders
The Black Hill Hotel Mystery
The Melton Lazars Mystery
The Woods of St Francis Mystery

By Way of Introduction

Freddie Cat

THIS IS AN INTRODUCTION WRITTEN by me, Freddie cat. I wrote it today. I write everything today as I live in the moment because I am a Buddhist cat. This is the third book in the series after *The Diary of a Buddhist Cat* and *Our Cats in Amsterdam*. The events described here take place immediately after the adventures in the second book.

I think this is the opportune time to remind you what happened in the first two books. In *The Diary of a Buddhist Cat*. I was saved from the cat shelter by my human parents Mary and John. A new life began. As I'm a Buddhist cat, I treat everything with respect – people, animals, birds, plants, even my breakfast. Then I met Gemma who was also saved from the shelter by Mary and John, though she didn't see things in the same way that I did when we first met. Gemma regarded humans as oppressors as they took her kittens. She also thought I was soft in the head, but I think she saw my approach brought rewards as I won friends, gained knowledge, stopped thieves, and even helped a squirrel fly further from a children's slide. During these activities I featured on social media. Therefore, to be on the safe side, I was dyed a butterscotch colour before I went out on the streets of Amsterdam.

This was because in *Our Cats in Amsterdam*, Gemma and I undertook some risky adventures following people who were involved in crimes like drugs – and people-trafficking. Gemma fought back against their activities by transferring money from their bank accounts to charities in the Netherlands and the UK. Gemma adapted to spying very well but had concerns that the people we helped capture might have friends who could harm our human parents, Mary and John. While we were away someone monitored the house and made sure that no one tried to break in. Our cat sitter, Mrs Elkins, also visited every day and moved two toy cats around inside to make it look as though we were in residence.

Now read on…

Chapter 1

Today

HELLO – WELCOME DEAR READER.

We arrive back at our home in the late afternoon with about twelve hours to spare before our human parents come back, at least according to the schedule that our minder Mrs Elkins shows us. The journey back was uneventful, although saying 'tot ziens' to Miep at Brussels was quite difficult. She was wonderful to us, and we will miss her, although I have this intuition that we'll work together again. Miep is the big boss for Europol in Amsterdam, and I reckon we'll be back there soon and who knows what Europol will need us to investigate?

For now, we must concentrate on getting back to normal and making things appear as though we've been at home for the last two weeks, when we haven't been at home for the last two weeks. Do you see what I mean? Mrs Elkins, who brought us back from Brussels on the Eurostar, has taken our carriers, the two toys, and a suitable amount of food and cat litter to cover our tracks.

Mrs Elkins also shows us the fridge, which contains a large cartwheel of cheese two feet across which Henk promised to send us. Henk is a crow who works for Europol and was our main animal contact in the Netherlands. We are now primed for John and Mary's return early tomorrow morning.

Gemma is downstairs having a nap. I'm reading a book called *Primitive Rebels* by Eric Hobsbawn, a famous historian who is thorough in his research with footnotes on most pages. Eric is writing about individuals and groups who've been rebellious at local levels in Sicily and Andalusia in Spain. These groups are mostly socialists and anarchists. As Eric indicates, being an anarchist means you're against any kind of organised state. The socialists were interested in everyone working hard and owning an equal share of property and the results of their labours. The authorities weren't keen on these ideas and stamped out the local rebellions as and when they happened.

Gemma would enjoy this book, and it might inspire her to organise a protest against tree vandalism by the council in the local park. I fall asleep reading about city mobs and dream about being chased over canal bridges by people throwing clogs, tulips, and small windmills at me. I have to apologise as my dreams appear to bring out my stereotypical thinking about places.

Chapter 2

Today

I WAKE UP THIS MORNING to a familiar smell and a familiar noise. The smell is the coffee that I presume John has put on in order to wake him up. The noise is him lurching around in his bedroom, trying not to trip over the furniture and failing by the sounds of it. I think he is unpacking his suitcase too, and it sounds like it's fighting back.

I pad softly over to the door of his room and peer inside. It appears I wasn't the only one dyed on holiday. John has also changed colour. He's now a sort of pink colour, at least on his face, arms, and legs. It doesn't suit him as he's now the colour of lobsters. Whoever painted him that colour in the Maldives has forgotten to return him to his normal skin colour. I wonder why John was undercover on an Indian Ocean island disguised as a lobster. I decide to trot downstairs for a poo and a snack. Gemma is already eating the remains of her supper from the previous today.

"Good morning," says Gemma. "Mary and John are back from their holidays. Mary is still asleep, but I can hear John is awake and stumbling around upstairs."

"Yes, he's been undercover," I reply. "The people in the

Maldives dyed him a different colour, a sort of pink colour like salmon or lobster."

Gemma narrows her eyes – "I think he's probably sunburnt, Freddie. Humans can't stay in strong sunshine for any length of time without putting on the right strength of suntan lotion."

"That must be painful," I say. "We should be thankful we don't get sunburnt, Gemma."

"I suppose so. I think pigs get sunburned too, but that's it I believe."

"I didn't know pigs sunbathed, but I suppose they can do what they want," I reply and finish my kibbles before trotting upstairs. I look out of the window and see Holly running in her wheel and the crows meandering about on the lawn looking for snacks. Today is a day when my human parents would normally go to work, but this day is different as they will wash their clothes and unpack all the items they took on holiday, most of which they probably didn't use.

I sit on the wooden chair in the kitchen and wait for the actors in the play to come onto the stage. I'm also interested to see how they react when they see the cheese in the fridge. John comes into the kitchen and wanders past me to get to the coffee machine. He pours most of it into a cup and then takes a slurp. He is still a strange pink colour, and he keeps rubbing his skin as I presume it itches. Then he notices me and comes over to the chair to give me a stroke.

"I got sunburned, Fred," he says, "two days ago, I fell asleep in the sun, and I hadn't put on any suntan lotion. Mary was windsurfing and didn't get back until it was too late."

I miaow in sympathy.

John moves across to the fridge and opens the door.

"Do you know when this arrived?" he asks.

I have a minor role to play now and must act as though I do not know what is in the fridge. I drop onto the floor and creep slowly towards the door and peer inside. The cheese is still sitting in red-wax splendour on the middle shelf, occupying most of the space. I look at the cheese and then look at John. I miaow because I do not know when this arrived. This is the truth.

At this time, Mary appears in the kitchen and wanders over to see what we're looking at.

"Wow, when did this arrive?" she asks. "There's a note attached to it." She picks up the cream-coloured envelope and opens it.

"Congratulations, your email address was selected ahead of fifty thousand others to receive this Gouda cheese. Enjoy the taste of the Netherlands. Henk."

"Who's Henk?" asks John.

"Someone who knows how to find out our postal address from our email address," replies Mary, "and I wonder which draw this was? I don't remember entering a draw to win a cheese, large or small. Did you, John? By the way, your skin looks worse now than it did two days ago."

"I've put on half a bottle of after-sun cream this morning," replies John, "the type that's supposed to draw the heat out of the skin, so I hope it will calm down today. As for the cheese, I don't enter contests to win food, so it wasn't me, but I will help you eat it as I like Gouda, especially on toast."

Gemma chooses this moment to appear in the kitchen doorway and pads over to where I'm sitting.

"Hello, Gemma," says Mary, stroking Gemma on the top of the head.

"They've found the cheese then," says Gemma, glancing at Mary. "Have they said anything about the Netherlands?"

"No, but neither of them can remember entering the contest to win the cheese."

"Well, there's a reason for that, isn't there?" replies Gemma, deciding she'll rub herself around Mary's legs as a thank you for the stroke on the head.

"Yes, how did they find out about the email address?" I ask.

"From Mrs Elkins, I presume," replies Gemma, "it was on the piece of paper that Mary handed over to her just before they left."

"I wouldn't rub around John's legs," I say. "He's put on some lotion that is supposed to help him with his sunburn."

"Thank you, that stuff would taste terrible when I wash my fur, anyway I will see you later." Gemma trots away, avoiding John's attempt at a stroke.

Mary and John pull the cheese out of the fridge and are inspecting it with some interest.

"There's plenty of cheese for us for a few weeks," says Mary. "I suppose I'll like this type of cheese by the time we finish it."

"Right, I suppose so. Anyway, I should get the washing done. It would be great to start off our work week tomorrow with a full complement of clean clothes." With that, he ambles off downstairs to the washing machine and dryer. Mary places the cheese on the kitchen counter as they will go out later to do the food shopping and need an emptier fridge.

I retire to the underneath of the couch and finish the book *The Roots of Coincidence* by Arthur Koestler. This is a wonderful book and makes me realise how little I know, and humans know about the world we inhabit. For many decades, extra-sensory perception (ESP) – including clairvoyance and telepathy – has been dismissed as illusion and fakery. ESP was compared with the world of physics, as scientists thought it existed, and dismissed as unimportant and contradictory to the established scientific norms.

But nowadays, with Quantum Physics breaking the established models of nature and the universe and introducing concepts such as particles travelling backwards in time and electrons being both a wave and a particle depending on whether they're observed, ESP fits in more easily.

This book suggests it's time for a new attitude towards parapsychology and that there is a natural law that leads to coincidences occurring.

Our world is strange indeed and maybe ESP is the least strange of all the phenomena in our existence. The book doesn't mention whether a Buddhist or a Buddhist cat could conduct a test to see whether they can receive thoughts from other people.

I try some ESP when Mary and John go shopping and send them kind thoughts about buying cat food containing fish oil or Omega-3 oil to improve my memory. I'm not sure if that's being selfish or not? It would help Gemma too, not that her memory isn't excellent already, especially in relation to bank accounts and the names of charities.

In connection with this wish, I decide to read *Why Has Nobody Told Me This Before?* by Dr Julie Smith, who is a clinical psychologist who helps people understand their lives and why they have the thoughts they do. It appears most thoughts come into our minds whether we want them to or not, so we have to learn to evaluate our thoughts and discard the ones we don't want. Thoughts are not facts. With this thought, I drift off to sleep, and that's a fact. I'm looking forward to the next day, as I will go out and see my friends in the garden and perhaps in the park too.

Chapter 3

Today

IT'S A GREY DAY OUTSIDE and rain is falling steadily. I peer through the blinds. There are clear skies heading our way, so I hope when I go outside after my respectful breakfast that it won't be too wet. Stan, Sid, and Seb are looking for food – they've swapped the park for the garden – and Reg and his family have moved over to the park. John is stomping around in his bedroom, heading to work. The aroma of percolating coffee fills the lounge and seems to wake me up. I trot downstairs to find that our litter trays have been cleaned. There's a generous pile of kibbles in our bowls, plus some wet food. On the shelf above there are new tins of cat food, ten of them. I jump up for a closer inspection. I'm pleased to say that these tins contain some essential fish oils. Well, who'd have thought it, apart from me, of course? Does this mean I have ESP or were Mary and John going to buy these tins anyway, even without my potential intervention?

"Good morning, Freddie," says Gemma, "what are you doing up there?"

"I'm finding out if my attempt at ESP yesterday has worked, Gemma."

"What attempt at ESP was that?"

"I wanted to see whether they would buy some cat food containing essential oils to improve our memory, and they appear to have done so."

"Well, how do you know they weren't going to buy those same tins anyway?" says Gemma, looking at me with her most plausible look.

"I don't," I reply, "but the fact is, Mary and John bought appropriate tins of cat food."

"If you really want to practise your ESP, Frederick, transmit a thought asking them to buy something they rarely buy, such as an inflatable ostrich, an elephant trap, or a blue banana."

"Those items are unavailable in most supermarkets, Gemma. That's not a proper test. We should choose items readily available in supermarkets, such as a slice of watermelon or a bunch of garlic. Items Mary and John don't normally buy."

Gemma smiles – "Okay, we'll play a little game. When they go shopping next, you transmit thoughts about onions, and I'll transmit thoughts about garlic, and we'll see what happens. Let's hope we're not both successful, otherwise the smell of pungent food will be all around."

"Garlic is supposed to be good for us," I say. "I'm not sure of the best way to transmit thoughts to a human. I repeated the phrase 'cat food with essential oils' over and over in my mind and stared at them as they left. Is that what you should do?"

"I'm not sure," replies Gemma, "but that sounds right. Concentrate on, in my case, garlic and try to project that thought of garlic to them by looking at them with great intensity."

"That sounds like a good idea," I say, before jumping down and beginning to eat my breakfast with a gentle nod to my bowls of food.

"Are you practising ESP on me?" asks Gemma.

"No, I'm not," I reply. "Why? Have you been receiving strange thoughts?"

"Well, sort of, about which books I should read. I want to read an Agatha Christie book, perhaps the *Murder of Roger Ackroyd* or *The Hollow* or *Cat Among the Pigeons*."

"I've read those," I reply, "and they're all good, but in *Cat Among the Pigeons*, there's no cat and no pigeons."

"That's disgraceful," says Gemma. "We should sue Agatha under the Trade Descriptions Act. It's a misleading title. It will act like a magnet for all cat lovers and cats who can read. Then, lo-and-behold, there's no cat in the book. What are people supposed to do?"

"Not to mention pigeon fanciers and pigeons who can read, Gemma."

"Indeed, Freddie."

"The thing is, cats can't sue anyone under the law, as we won't be able to hire a lawyer and provide them with the reason for the lawsuit against Agatha's estate."

"That's a technicality," replies Gemma. "I'm going to send them an email. I can type after all and complain that way. If you buy *Animal Farm*, you expect there'll be a farm with animals on it as at least part of the story. George didn't disappoint us."

"Well, it's up to you. You should do as you indicate and see what they say by way of reply."

"I will, don't worry," she replies and trots off, having eaten just a few kibbles and three mouthfuls of wet food.

I do admire how decisive Gemma is and I realise I should try and be decisive too, when the situation calls for it. I head upstairs and sit on the kitchen chair as John and Mary move around the kitchen without their usual pre-work precision as they're out of practice, a sign that their holiday was a success. John is less pink than he was, and Mary doesn't comb her hair as much as normal. I'm relieved the kitchen window is open wide enough for me to slide through, and I head that way as soon as Mary and John depart.

I say 'Good Morning' to the cacti and the primroses on the window ledge and then climb down the trellis. I can feel the metal digging into my pads ever so slightly as the skin has become softer during my Amsterdam stay. The leaves of the rose flutter by way of welcome and I whisper, 'It's good to see you too' by way of return.

"Freddie," says Stan, "how are you? You're looking well."

"I feel refreshed," I say, "but it's wonderful to see you all – how have things been when we were away? How are you all?"

"Well," says Seb, "we're all doing well. Thank you for asking. I'm pleased to be talking to you rather than the stuffed toy the housekeeper left in the window. She moved you both around quite a bit and you always appeared in different windows every day, so she must have been keeping a record of where she placed you. Occasionally, you and Gemma were in the same window, which looked rather odd."

"That's interesting," I reply. "I doubt Gemma and I have ever sat in the same window at the same time. Thank you for making it look as though we were imprisoned and couldn't come outside."

"You're welcome," says Sid, "your cat sitter seemed to be here most of the day during the week and she popped in for a couple of hours at the weekend, so she was dedicated to her task."

"She was kind," I say. "She looked after us well on our journey to Brussels."

"What did you do in Amsterdam?" asks Stan.

"We followed some people around, and some criminals were arrested and Gemma made quite a few charitable donations, including to the Royal Society for the Protection of Birds. Amsterdam is nice, with lots of museums and canals and people on bicycles. The squirrels over there watched videos of Rufus playing on the children's slide and landing on his face and admired his persistence. The crows are organised and receive help from parakeets."

"It sounds lovely," says Jacqueline, "we were concerned on the last two days before you came back, as someone watched your house. He was sitting in a car on the opposite side of the road and looking across here every so often."

"What did he look like?" I ask anxiously.

"He was a white man in a smart blue jumper, and he wore jeans. He was in a BMW, a red one, and he used to drive off for an hour and then come back but park in a different place," replies Jacqueline, "he sometimes parked in the library car park and looked across here."

"Is he around now?" I ask, "I hope he's not from the Dutch underworld and has come to whack myself and Gemma or our human parents."

"Wouldn't the Dutch underworld have whacked you in Amsterdam?" asks Stan. "How would they find out your address?"

"There was a sort of double-agent, a kingfisher called Frank, who tried to betray me by flapping his wings so some large dogs could assassinate me by pushing me in the canal, but they missed," I say, shivering slightly at the memory, "so he might have provided my home address, although I doubt he'd be able to find out that information."

"It sounds like you were in danger, Freddie," says Seb, "but the man in the car didn't keep a dog with him. I witnessed nothing that looked dangerous."

"There's nothing to worry about," says Jacqueline.

"I'm not worried about Gemma and me, so much as Mary and John, who don't even know where we went."

"They'll be okay," says Seb, "they'll soon sense something is wrong if they find someone hanging around they don't recognise."

"Well, I hope you're correct when you say that," I reply.

"There's something else," says Andrea, "the council still wants to chop that tree down in the park even though the wasps departed recently. I'm not sure I understand humans."

"We'll hug the tree, so they don't do that," I say. "Do you know the date when that's going to happen?"

"It's later this week," replies Jacqueline, "tomorrow, in fact."

"Oh, thank you for letting me know," I say. "I should go over to the park and discover what's happening. I'm not sure why the council would want to chop down the tree. That's not nice of them. We should protest."

"I agree," says Stan, "we'll come and support you, of course. We need places to perch, as do the other small birds in the park."

"Will they help? The sparrows, the starlings, and the finches?"

"I'm sure they'll help us, especially if you talk to them in your usual kind voice."

"I'll do my best, as my mum always encouraged me to do," I say.

"I'm sure you will," says Andrea. "Rufus is getting ready to go over to the park, so you should go with him across the road. We'll fly over."

"Thank you, Andrea, I'd lost track of the time. I'd better scamper, as I'm not sure Rufus knows we're back. I'll see you over in the park." With that, I run over to the base of the tree in the front garden. Rufus is heading down to the ground.

"Freddie!! You're back. How are you?" Rufus is pleased to see me.

"I'm well, thank you. How are you?"

"I'm doing well, but I can't do a proper somersault yet, even off a low branch. I reckon it's my tail again. It seems to get in the way and weighs me down."

"Rufus, you don't have to do a somersault. You're famous already in the Netherlands. The squirrels in Amsterdam send their regards. They admire the way you fly, land on your face, but get up and do it all again."

"Oh! I never imagined that would happen. Was it the video the lady from the council took of me?"

"There are over a dozen videos, taken by different people. You're a social media star."

"Well, in that case, I must stay ahead of the game, which means perfecting that somersault technique. As I said, I'm landing on my tail instead of on my feet, so I'm not that far away, I suppose."

"That's positive thinking," I say. "Just rotate a little more and you'll make it."

"Yes, it's not much of a change to make. Did anyone mention me in Belgium? Or in France?"

"I didn't speak to any animals in either of those countries, as we were on the train."

"Well, those are other markets for me to become popular in. Perhaps the Belgians like somersaults? Or the French do? Anyway, we should head across the road, Freddie, and see what the park looks like today."

"Yes, let's do that, I want to check on the tree the wasps used to live in."

"Okay," says Rufus, "let's be very careful crossing the road. There's been someone looking at your house from a car for the last few days. I'm not sure what he was doing. He's not here today, by the looks of it. Right, let's go, there's no cars coming."

Rufus flops across the road and I scoot across as I don't trust the car-driving humans. I am wondering who the person in the car is and why they arrived while we were away. The park looks lovely, and I see the tree under threat is still where it should be. This is good news. The grass is looking a little parched, but the sprinklers seem to have positive effects on the two football pitches. Rufus heads away to the yellow-coloured slide and I trot over to the tree.

"Hello, Freddie," says Reg the crow, "how are you? Welcome back."

"Hello, Reg," I reply, "I'm fine, thank you for asking. How are you all?"

"We're all doing well, thank you. We're concerned about the tree. It's everyone's favourite perching tree, but the council are determined to chop it down."

"Oh no, that's not good. Have they put another notice on it?"

"Yes, tomorrow is the day, apparently."

"Oh, I'd better get Gemma over here tomorrow and we'll hug the tree in solidarity. Or climb up it and grab a branch each."

"We'll perch on the branches with you," says Reg, "and here's the rest of us."

The rest of the crows land around us. I stand on my back legs and wave at them all with my front paws, a trick I learned in Amsterdam. When I glance towards the upper part of the park, I think I can see another cat.

"Who is that up there?" I ask.

"Where?" says Rob, looking around to where I'm pointing.

"It's a cat I've not seen before," I reply. "I should say hello. He just appeared at the top of the park."

"He's been around for a few days," says Ron, "he keeps himself to himself."

"I'll talk to him. Perhaps he can help with the tree," I say and scamper off towards the top of the park. It's time to be decisive and help this cat.

As I approach the cat, I notice he's still quite young. He has a white bib, but the rest of him is jet black.

"Hello," I say, "I'm Freddie, what's your name?"

The cat looks down at the ground before mumbling, "Oliver, my name's Oliver."

"That's a nice name, Oliver."

"Is it?" says Oliver, glancing at me before looking away. "I don't like it myself. It sounds weak and effeminate, especially if people call me Olly. I don't like being called Olly."

"Well, Oliver, what are you doing in the park? Are you having a look around?"

"Well, to tell the truth, I'm feeling listless, Freddie. I'm looking for something to do, to give me a sense of purpose."

"Oliver, we were meant to meet here today. I have something that I hope might interest you. There's a tree down there that the council wants to remove, and we should stop them."

"That sounds like something I could do," says Oliver. "I enjoy jumping into trees and climbing them."

"Excellent," I say, "come and meet my crow friends. There are a lot of them, but don't let that worry you, Oliver. They're friendly."

"That sounds good," says Oliver, perking up a little. "I'd

like to meet them, but I am shy of crowds normally, so I hope everything goes well."

"It will do," I say, "and don't worry, all you can do is to be yourself. Don't be someone you're not."

"Well, you say that, but I'd prefer to be called Bertram, which can be shortened to Bert, or Bartholomew, which can be shortened to Bart. They sound more masculine than Olly does."

"Oliver is a perfectly good masculine name, but if you want to make it into a name that you think sounds masculine, how about Iver? How does that sound?"

"Oh, Iver sounds quite cool, actually, I like that... I'm Iver... yes sounds good, thank you."

"You're welcome. Now let's visit my friends. I'll introduce you as Iver."

Oliver and I trot down to where the crows have been watching us.

"Ladies and gentlemen, this is my new friend, Oliver, who goes by the name of Iver."

"Welcome, Iver," says the crows in unison, and then they introduce themselves individually.

"Hello, everyone," says Oliver. "I'm pleased to meet you all. I've just moved in with my human parents into the house overlooking the park with the lilac tree in the front garden."

"They enjoy gardening, don't they?" says Rob, "they really do, planting lots of bulbs. I've seen them on their knees in the soil, spacing the bulbs at regular intervals."

"They do like digging around in the soil," replies Oliver, "but the garden will be picturesque when they've finished."

"Well, we will visit," says Reg, "it sounds like there'll be plenty of insects and worms for us, because your humans will keep the soil in good condition."

"Well, they're keen at the moment," says Oliver, "and I hope they continue, as I would like a nice, colourful garden to look at from the window."

"I think we should talk about this tree," says Stan pointing with his wing, "according to this notice, the council will be 'assessing' the tree tomorrow, or on the next today if you're a Buddhist, at 10:30am and might chop it down."

I give a brief nod to Stan for his kind consideration.

"Who's a Buddhist?" asks Oliver.

"I am," I say. "Stan was being deferential towards me. I regard every day as today and I try not to think of yesterday and tomorrow."

"That's great," says Oliver. "I like the sound of Buddhism."

"The thing is," continues Stan, "what shall we do tomorrow to show the council we want them to reconsider their decision?"

"We should take action," says Rob, "perhaps fly around their heads so they aren't comfortable doing their assessment."

"Look over there," says Seb, "there's that Penny lady with her little dog, Duchess, walking on the edge of the park. I wonder how long it will be before she takes out her phone and comes to film us."

"Oh, I have an idea," says Jacqueline, "let's encourage her to film us, so hopefully tomorrow she'll do the same when we have our protest."

"Yes, great idea," I say. "I read something in a marketing book about taking hold of the narrative. If we bother the council employees, then the story will be about animals attacking employees going about their business, but if we stand in front of the tree…"

"…or in the tree…" interjects Oliver.

"…or in the tree, yes, in the tree… good point… we'll make the story about animals occupying a tree so that the humans will understand what we're doing and know we don't want the tree chopped down."

"That's a great idea," says Rob, "and then Penny could film us and show it to her friends, and we'd have some free publicity."

"But if she films us today and shows it to people, perhaps more humans will arrive tomorrow and see us in the tree," continues Oliver.

"Even the TV Networks might be interested," I say, "wouldn't that be great, to see ourselves on the television?"

"That's not a problem we'd have," says Rob, "unless you could record it for us, Freddie, and then show us at a later time?"

"Of course, I'd be delighted to," I say, realising as I say it I'm not sure how to record a TV show. I'm sure Gemma will know, so I'll ask her later.

"Penny's coming this way," says Rob, "I hope Rufus keeps out of sight, as we don't want Penny's dog Duchess to take fright and leave, otherwise Penny might not video us."

"I'll warn him to stay out-of-sight on the slide until later," says Jacqueline, flying off towards the children's playground.

Penny moves cautiously towards us. Her little dog gains some confidence when it sees that the crows and cats aren't menacing. I feel sure that she will soon recognise me and so I decide not to hide, but to draw her attention to the council's poster.

"It's Freddie," says Penny, "your owners must be back."

I miaow in agreement. She is correct on both counts. I point at the poster on the tree.

"What's this... the council are going to chop the tree down. That's not right. The tree looks good to me."

I place my paws around the tree as far as they'll go. This isn't far as my front legs are stubby.

"Aw, you're hugging the tree," says Penny, videoing me with some enthusiasm. Oliver jumps into the tree and, taking their cue from him, the crows land on the branches.

"Is this an animal protest?" asks Penny. "I shall have to send this video to the city news team. I'm guessing you're coming back tomorrow to show the council that you don't want the tree to be chopped down."

I miaow and the crows caw. Oliver purrs.

"This is great, thank you," says Penny. Duchess stands by the tree and gives a little bark. Penny films this too. I'm pleased Duchess has gained some confidence from her visit today. I wonder if any television crews will arrive tomorrow, as the publicity would be wonderful for the tree. Penny replays the video on her phone and seems satisfied. She eases Duchess away from the tree. The little dog looks at me and the crows and trots off with a spring in her step. I reckon she will drag her owner over to the tree tomorrow. Oliver is still purring and enjoying the view. As Duchess has gone, Rufus heads over towards us, accompanied by Jacqueline.

"Hello, everyone, are you practising your protest for tomorrow?" he asks.

"Well, that wasn't the intention at first, but Penny can provide some valuable publicity if she sends off the video," I explain, "and that might save this tree from a sad fate. Her little dog was gaining confidence as well, which is good."

"It is," replies Rufus, "but I'm worried she'd run off if she saw me, so I'd better keep away tomorrow, as we need the publicity to make sure the tree isn't chopped down."

"That's considerate of you, Rufus," says Stan, "but it probably is the best course of action, as if Duchess takes fright, then Penny will leave too."

"We could dye you another colour," I say, "that happened to me in the Netherlands, to stop people recognising me, but we'd need a human to do that."

"Oh, I'm quite happy with the colour I am. I'll practise on the slide when your protest or eco-action, as it should be called, is taking place. Perhaps we can connect the slide to the tree somehow?"

"I'm not sure how," says Rob. "It would detract from the tree protest, wouldn't it, Rufus?"

"I was thinking," says Rufus, "that it would make the park a more appealing place for people to come to and the council would be in favour of that. Especially if they could watch the slide being used by a leaping squirrel."

"We could do that I'm sure," I say, "but it's more important to save the tree and then show the council how they can increase the appeal of the park by showing them your leaping skills."

"I suppose it would be more of a story for the TV," says Andrea, "if there was a squirrel jumping off a slide. There'd be more for the media to be interested in, and they might raise the profile of the park, making it more difficult for the council to be sneaky about chopping the tree down."

"That's true, Andrea," says Oliver. "Perhaps when the council people leave we could draw the attention of anyone with a camera to the slide where Rufus will be performing."

"That sounds like a good idea," says Rufus. "I'll watch for a signal from here and start leaping from the slide, and hopefully people will see me and their interest will be piqued."

"That sounds like a plan," says Stan, "so we should all meet here at 10am tomorrow and find out what the council does in terms of personnel."

"Yes, that sounds like a good idea," I say. "That will give us plenty of time to plan if anything strange appears to be happening."

"Yes, you never can be sure with humans," says Oliver. "They can sometimes change their minds quickly and for no apparent reason."

"You're very knowledgeable for a young cat, Iver," says Rob. "How do you know this?"

"Because my humans keep changing the position of my litter tray every week," replies Oliver, "it's by the wall one week and then in the middle of the room the following week and then back against the wall. It makes no difference to me. I just use it wherever it is, but they seem to move it every few days, simply because they can and for no other reason."

"That sounds right," says Rufus. "Have you ever tried a slide, Oliver?"

"I haven't," replies Oliver. "I don't like the idea of being out of control, of moving and not being able to stop."

"It doesn't last for very long," replies Rufus, "and all I do is concentrate on taking off at the right time."

"You'll soon stop when you hit the ground," says Seb, "but what you have to be careful about is how you land. It took Rufus a long time to perfect that, didn't it Rufus?"

"Yes, landing is difficult to control and as you might imagine, you can really hurt yourself, so I would advise you to take it easy at the start and don't hurl yourself down the slide straightaway."

"Oh," says Oliver, "there's another cat heading this way." Sure enough, Gemma is trotting down the grassy incline past two small rhododendrons whose flowers are just coming out. She has a purpose about her that reminds me of her hurrying through the Vondelpark on our recent adventure in Amsterdam.

"It's Gemma," says Ron. "She must have got across the road with no problems."

"Who's Gemma?" asks Oliver.

"She lives with Freddie," replies Jacqueline, "isn't that right?"

"It is, Jacqueline," I say. "I'm surprised she's come across the road on her own, but I dare say she looked both ways and didn't cross when there were cars coming."

"Hello, everyone," says Gemma, trotting up to the group of us. "What news of the tree?"

"The council are coming tomorrow at 10:30am to inspect the tree," says Oliver.

"Sorry. Who are you?" asks Gemma, with only a slightly icy tone.

"I'm Oliver," says Iver, "but I prefer to be called Iver and not Olly."

"Oh, that's such a shame," replies Gemma. "I do like the name Olly. It flows off the tongue so well, my tongue I mean, not necessarily anyone else's tongue. Olly sounds fine to me, but obviously I will abide by your wishes. Anyway, the council is coming tomorrow and we're going to hug the tree."

"We're going to occupy the tree," I say, "with the help of the crows and other birds and Penny is going to video us and other local news organisations will also come to the park because she'll send them the video she took a few minutes ago."

"Right," says Gemma, "well that all sounds wonderful, and what will the squirrel be doing?"

"Rufus is going to be over on the slide as we don't want Penny's dog, Duchess, getting scared of Rufus and running off. Once the council goes, Rufus can jump down the slide and the news channels will film that too, as it's an unusual occurrence, wouldn't you say?"

"This all sounds excellent to me," says Gemma. "It's good to make the park an interesting place for humans to come to and spend their time, although we should try not to turn it into an outdoor circus. The more publicity, the better. I can't wait to discover the expressions on the faces of the council's representatives when they find cats in a tree along with crows."

"They wouldn't chop down the tree with us in it, would they?" asks Oliver.

"Well, if it's being filmed then I would doubt it, Oll... sorry Iver," says Gemma, "but with humans you never can tell what they'll do. Expect the unexpected."

"Do you want to have a go on the slide, Gemma?" asks Rufus. "Iver does and we've got a bit of time before I go back, so I could help you if you want to slide down."

"I'll try it," says Gemma, "though I might be slow at first, until I gain some confidence. Perhaps Iver should go first."

We trot across the slightly brown grass towards the slide with a slight breeze blowing in our faces. The trees in this area seem less healthy than the tree that's bothering the council. They need some water as their leaves are going brown at the edges. Iver leaps onto the top of the slide and has a quick look downwards before launching himself towards the ground on his back. When he flies off the end, he performs a somersault and lands on his feet.

"He did a somersault," says Rufus. "He did a somersault without even trying. That's incredible."

"He did it without thinking," I say, "which is different and is why he could do it. You're probably overthinking it, plus he went down tail first and you descend headfirst."

"Yes, you're right," says Rufus. "I'm going to try that. Oh, he's having another go. He's keen... that one didn't go so well."

Iver had spun around slightly too much and landed hard on his back legs, jolting him. The grass in the landing area is compact from people landing on it.

Gemma climbs up to the top of the slide and puts her paws out in front of her as she slides down so that she drops off the end of the slide rather than flying for any length of time.

She walks over to me: "Did I do something wrong? Shouldn't I have flown further than that? I just dropped off the end."

"Your paws were acting as brakes all the way down," I explain. "Lift them all up and slide on your back. You have less control that way, but more speed. Or you can use the Rufus method of headfirst and lift your paws to the side slightly."

"Right," says Gemma. "I'll try the sliding on the back method and use my tail to rotate me onto my paws before landing. That's if I have time to remember to do all that."

Gemma pats Iver on the head in a not too affectionate way. He's still recuperating from his jolt and is walking around gingerly, making sure everything is in working order. Gemma climbs up the steps and positions herself carefully before starting her run. She flies off the end of the slide and sticks her tail out, which corrects her rotation, and she lands on front paws with her rear paws hitting the ground a second later.

"Oh well, that felt quite exhilarating," says Gemma. "I can understand why the squirrel keeps doing it."

"Gemma, his name is Rufus, not 'The Squirrel'. I'm not sure why you can't remember that."

"Yes, that's right, I should call him by his name. You're

right. Rufus is his name. Anyway, that's enough flying for one day. Perhaps tomorrow, we should use the slide too, to keep the media's attention on the park."

"That's a great idea," I reply. "The more animals that use the slide, the more publicity we'll get."

"You realise that if the news networks grace the park with their presence, our humans will almost certainly see us on the news, and then it will be interesting to discover what they do."

"They'll support us, Gemma. Perhaps they'll come over and stand with us and make sure the tree is saved."

"Yes, you might be right, Freddie. There's something else though, isn't there? Those people we followed in Amsterdam, they might have friends who could recognise us if they watch TV. You know how many cat videos there are – thousands of them, so we should be careful when we're going about our business."

"The crows were saying there was someone watching the house from a car during our time away," I say. "But this person stayed in their car and didn't approach the house at all."

"I see," replies Gemma. "That person might have been on our side making sure no one came to the house when we were away. I think that's the case, perhaps when Mrs Elkins wasn't here?"

"I hope that's correct. I wonder if Aubrey and Arabella would know?"

"Let's ask Stan and Ron whether they know if their cousins are coming to see us."

After giving one of her front paws a quick lick because a

speck of dirt had dared to attach itself to her, Gemma scampers over to the crows, closely followed by me.

"Hello, Stan," says Gemma, "do you know if your cousins Aub and Arabella are coming to see us in the next few days?"

"I think Rob knows more than I do, as he's our contact on the crow grapevine," replies Stan, looking at Rob.

"Yes, Gemma," says Rob, "they are coming to see you for a debriefing session, but I'm not completely sure when yet. You had a problem with a kingfisher from what they said, so they're trying to find out what that means for security before coming here in an official capacity. I think it might be the day after tomorrow before they're here."

"Thank you, Rob," says Gemma, and appears worried.

"Try not to be anxious," I say. "No one's going to harm us here."

"We don't know that. Those people we followed could have violent friends in this country who don't like cats. Or they might harm Mary and John, who don't even know we were away and would be innocent of any wrongdoing."

"I think you're worrying about things that are unlikely to happen, but let's discover what Aubrey and Arabella say when they arrive. You should remember your Stoic books and try to deal with events when they arrive, and not before."

"Yes, you're right, I should do that, I should remember and not react. Anyway, the people in the Netherlands wouldn't know our address, would they? Miep from Europol met us in Brussels."

"Is everything okay?" asks Iver.

"Yes, we were just talking about our recent adventure,"

says Gemma, "and two of our crow friends are coming to see us the day after tomorrow."

"How are you, Iver?" I ask. "You landed with a jolt the last time you used the slide."

"Yes, I can still feel it," says Oliver. "I think Rufus is very brave to keep jumping the way he does."

"He's better than he used to be," says Gemma. "He always used to land on his face, but now he lands on his paws instead. His face is very pleased about that."

"I'll bet it is. Anyway, I will go back to my home. My owners get upset if I stay out too long. I will see you here tomorrow."

"'Bye, Iver," say Gemma and I in unison. We watch as Iver waves to the crows and heads up a small incline before heading across the grass towards the trees on the edge of the park. He looks both ways before going across the road and through a black garden gate.

"I hope it's a coincidence he's arrived just as we've returned from Amsterdam," says Gemma.

"You're concocting another conspiracy theory. You should leave that to people who have nothing better to do with their time."

"I have a suspicious mind, I think that's what it is, a suspicious mind, the kind of mind that's always asking – what if? What if Oliver is here to monitor us?"

"Cats don't buy houses, humans do."

"Maybe Olly's humans are part of the same gang of people as those people we followed in the Netherlands."

"Breathe and try to concentrate on your breathing and

forget this idea. Oliver and his humans moved in before we headed over to the Netherlands."

"Are you sure? If that's the case, then I have nothing to worry about, do I? I was just being silly."

"The visit of Aubrey and Arabella can't come soon enough," I say. I decide to change the subject – "How did you find crossing the road this morning?"

"It wasn't too bad, there were no cars coming in either direction, so I could stroll across. I can see why Rufus goes at that time. It's not rush hour and most of the drivers are taking their time, as they're heading to work."

"Let's hope it's like that when we go back," I say. "Did you want to go back now, or should we wait for Rufus?"

"Well, Rufus is serious about his cat-escorting duties. We should wait for him. We don't want him getting upset with us, do we?"

"Rufus has our safety at heart. He takes responsibility for that, which is nice of him."

"Rufus is a good flyer, but not so good at somersaults," replies Gemma, watching Rufus land awkwardly after a near complete rotation.

"He'll get there; he's obsessed with getting better and he'll improve."

"About tomorrow. What should we do if Mary and John spy us on the news?"

"Well, we can't do anything. They'll be concerned that we cross that road, so they might keep the windows closed for what they reckon is our own protection."

"I'm not sure they'll do that," says Gemma. "They like

their fresh air too much, but they might close them more tightly so that we can't get through."

"Yes, and neither of us would like that, but we mustn't think only of ourselves, Gemma. That tree is more important than us and should be our priority."

"Well, folks," says Rufus, "I've done enough jumps for one day. We should head back and get some rest before the big day tomorrow. I'm famished and need some food."

"Yes, that's a good idea, Rufus," says Gemma. "Lead the way and we'll follow you as we want to get back safely to the other side of the road."

"Of course," says Rufus, "and I'll choose a suitable spot, so we can all see both ways and cross with no risk."

==========

After eating a quick snack, I decide to finish a book called *The Fifth Child* by Doris Lessing, which I'd started the previous day. I have to say it's a good story about a selfish couple called David and Harriet who buy a big house and intend to have eight children. Luckily for them, the husband has a rich father, and the wife has a doting mother. The rich father pays their mortgage, the doting mother looks after the children. There are big family gatherings with stepfathers, stepmothers, sisters, cousins, nephews, and nieces. This is a privileged family indeed.

Then the fifth child arrives, a goblin called Ben.

Everything changes.

Harriet and David can't control Ben. He murders a dog, a cat, and tries to kill his brother Paul. This is where the story becomes ludicrous, because all this 'bad behaviour' is tolerated until it gets too much. Ben is carted off, having broken up the family, to a strange children's hospital up north where it rains all the time and there are moors! How stereotypical is that?

After Mary and John come home from work, they tell us all about their holidays in the Maldives. Gemma stares at them as she sits on the couch and listens as they recount how they swam a lot, ate a large amount of fresh fruit and vegetables, and sunbathed too much. I miaow my encouragement at intervals because they enjoyed themselves and look enthused when recounting their tales. Gemma looks guilty and glances at me as though she wishes she could tell them about our adventure. I wonder if she'll try to hint about the holiday by standing on the large cheese at the first available opportunity. They also bought presents for us, some small blankets made of cotton, which they place on our beds. These small blankets smell clean and give me a good place to hide my book where my bed is located under the sofa.

Mary and John go to bed earlier than normal as they're feeling tired and are suffering from jet lag because of the change in time zones. This gives me time to read a book called *A Short History of Myth* about myths through the ages from the earliest days of humankind. The author is Karen Armstrong, who was once a nun but escaped to write her eloquent books on a variety of religious and historical subjects.

I fall asleep and dream I'm painting pictures of birds and rodents on a wall in a house. I'm wearing a beret and smoking a cigarette and have my palette balanced on my paw. This painting takes place in the dark.

Chapter 4

Today

I WAKE UP HAVING CREATED a magnificent painted room in my dream. Mice, rats, and a few birds covered the walls, even though I've caught none of those creatures. I was venerating them in my dream, like the human hunters did in Palaeolithic times. I must now wake up because in the waking world, I must venerate a tree in the park and make sure it remains where it is for many years and isn't turned into wood chips or biomass by thoughtless humans.

After a stretch and reading some more of the myths book, my stomach rumbles, and I head downstairs to eat some breakfast respectfully. Gemma nods at me with a determined look in her eyes, and I smile. We eat in silence as the humans go about their pre-work routine upstairs. Gemma and I finish our breakfasts and head upstairs into the kitchen, where we sit under the wooden chair and keep our tails out of the way of John's heavy footsteps.

The window is open, which means we can head out after the humans have gone to work. John has burned his toast and left most of a slice on a light-green porcelain plate on the counter. I know some creatures that might like to eat that toast, and I try to work out how I can carry it outside without tasting the blackened bread. I thought toasters were foolproof.

"What are you kitties waiting for?" asks Mary suspiciously.

We miaow and head off into the lounge where we make a show of falling asleep on the couch. We yawn, stretch, and roll over a few times before closing our eyes. Mary eyes us before heading out of the back door to the garage.

"I suppose we should wait a few minutes before heading outside," says Gemma. "It would be ironic indeed if Mary saw us crossing the road and had an accident."

"We wouldn't want that," I say, "not today of all days when our destiny is to be in the park and protesting on behalf of the tree."

Gemma looks out of the window.

"There's someone sitting in a car on the opposite side of the road to our house and he keeps glancing over here."

"Is he looking anywhere else?" I ask.

"Not really, no. He looks straight ahead most of the time."

"He'll spy us if we go to the park our normal way," I say. "I'll have to organise a distraction."

"Crows?" says Gemma.

"Yes, I'll take that burnt toast to them and ask them to drop it on the car when I give the signal. When the man is out of his car, we can scoot across the road, and he won't see us."

"What about Rufus, our crossing guide?"

"I'll ask the crows to tell him what's going on and I'm

sure he'll understand. Right now, I'll talk to Reg or Ron, who will be in the garden, and I'll take the toast with me. I'll try to stay out of sight."

"Thank you, I'll stay here and watch our man out there to find out what he's up to."

"Okay, thank you. I'll try to be quick about it."

I scamper across the lounge floor and into the kitchen. I jump onto the counter and say, "Good Morning," to the primroses and cacti. The primroses nod in reply while the cacti brandish their spikes in a friendly manner. The weather looks cool and grey outside. I pick up the toast with my teeth and manoeuvre through the window before dropping the toast onto the grass. I say 'hello' to the Lancashire Rose before climbing down the trellis.

Rob and Ron are admiring the toast.

"Good morning is this for us?" asks Ron.

"Good morning, Ron and Rob. It is for you and the family. I was hoping you could use it for something first."

"Use it? You mean to distract the man in the car who's outside your house?" asks Rob. "He was the one who was here when you were away."

"Exactly that, thank you. Could you also tell Rufus we'll meet him over in the park? Gemma and I will sneak across the road when the man is distracted."

"We'll do that," says Rob. "When should we start the distraction?"

"In five minutes, I'll just get Gemma, and you should be able to start when we're both on the grass. Thank you."

I wave to Holly, the hamster who's running in her wheel,

and climb back up the trellis to fetch Gemma, who is still looking out of the window.

"Gemma, I've arranged a distraction for us. We should go."

"Good, well done. The man seems to be looking after our house in a way. He seems to look at the people who walk by more than the house itself. Perhaps he is on our side?"

"You might be correct. Rob was saying the man in the car is the man who was here when we were away, but we shouldn't assume anything about him until we've spoken to Aub and Arabella."

"Right, anyway, let's get some exercise. That will help me get rid of some of the tension I'm feeling. I suppose that's why humans have massages. Do you think there are any cat masseurs around here? They could ease away the tension too."

"I'm not aware of any, and they might do more harm than good if you can't show where it is you're feeling tense."

"True, anyway let's go, enough of me there's a tree to save."

Gemma jumps from the back of the couch onto one of the fluffy red cushions that contrast so well with the light-blue covering. She kneads the cushion for several seconds with her front paws, tensing and untensing her feet, releasing some of the tension in her front legs. She scampers across the lounge and into the kitchen, followed by me. We leave via the window and climb down the trellis to the grass.

The sentinel crow caws five times. We've been spotted. We creep across the grass to the front of the garden, so we have a view of the man in his car. The crows gather on the surrounding cars and then Stan gives a single caw. They all land on the roof of the car at the same moment and start tapping on the roof. The man looks up and then opens his door to find out what's going on. As he steps out onto the road, Jacqueline drops the toast on his head. He picks up the slice of toast and we take this as our cue, after checking both ways, to scoot across the road and up the grassy bank from where we observe the crows fly off towards us. The man looks at the toast on both sides before throwing it onto the grass. He gets back in the car. Jacqueline grabs the toast and heads into the park to enjoy a well-earned snack along with her family.

"I have to say the crows' distractions are imaginative," says Gemma. "Tapping on the roof like that must be like heavy hailstones falling on the metal – what a great idea."

We trot down the slope and the vista of the park opens up.

"There's a TV van parked at the top of the park and another one on the far side," says Gemma.

"Indeed, there is, well Penny must have sent off her videos to some wonderful effect. Well, it's time to think up some good excuses, because our humans are going to see this. One cameraman is panning around the park right now."

The crows are finishing the toast and some of the smaller birds are pecking at the remaining crumbs with great glee.

"Hello," I say, "the distraction worked. Thank you for your help. Who thought of the idea?"

"It was Rob," says Ron. "He's the resident brains in our family and the philosopher-in-chief."

"You're welcome," says Rob, "and thank you for the toast. I presume your humans don't know how to operate a toaster?"

"No, the male human isn't good in the morning at anything," says Gemma. "He's not a morning person."

"Yes, we see him going along the pavement in the morning and he's all over the place. Shoelace undone, shirt buttons done up oddly, yawning away," says Andrea.

"There's a cameraman over there," says Ron. "He was filming us earlier eating your human's toast. I wonder if that will get onto the local news this evening?"

"It might well do, in a setting the scene kind of way," says Gemma, "especially if you're filmed in the tree."

"Right," says Ron, "let us know if we are on TV. It would be great if we are recorded for posterity at least once in our lives."

"I'll record the local news on the humans' TV so we can see ourselves afterwards, during the day when the humans are out," replies Gemma.

"You know how to do that?" asks Stan.

"Oh yes, I watched the humans do it. You have to use the correct gizmo and press the green button, and it records everything. You then use another gizmo to access the recorded program."

"What is a gizmo?" asks Jacqueline.

"It's the name given by people to items of machinery that they don't know the name of," says Gemma, "In my example, I think the gizmo is in fact called the 'remote' because you can program the television from the comfort of your seat if you're a human that is."

"Oh, if we sat on your window ledge then you could turn the TV towards us and we could watch the screen," says Rob.

"It points in that direction anyway," says Andrea, "I noticed that when you were away, and the cat sitter pulled up the blind by pulling on the string."

"Oh yes," says Gemma, putting her right front paw on her head, "yes, I'd forgotten about that. The Venetian blinds in that front window are difficult to operate for us. The cords get stuck in our claws, but we'll have a go tomorrow and find out what we can do."

"Another TV van has parked," says Rob, "and there's another one behind it. And the council has just arrived."

"Penny is on the far side of the park with her dog," I say.

"Well, it's all happening now, because Rufus is here too," says Jacqueline.

"Therefore, it must be 10am," I say, "because Rufus is on time. The council will soon get ready to inspect the tree."

"And here is young Olly," says Gemma, "oh sorry, I should say 'Iver'."

Oliver comes bounding up to the group.

"Morning all," says Oliver, "there seems to be a lot of camera people around. The reporters are trying to find the right tree and get their camera angles sorted out."

"Good morning," says Rufus, who is breathless. "I'm going to head over to the slide once the council people get out of their vehicle."

"Sounds good. Start your flying once the council people are looking at us in the tree," says Rob.

"I'll do that," says Rufus. "Starting before then would be a distraction to the chief aim, which is saving that tree."

"A reporter is heading our way clutching a microphone," says Seb. "Will they try to interview us?"

"They could try," I say, "but it wouldn't be good human TV. Our answers would be predictable."

"There's another van with a logo on the side," says Jacqueline. "It's a TV company too. That's six now."

"We should move towards the tree and see what happens," I say. "Let's find out how many reporters there are. The council people appear to be about to move or they're thinking about moving, so it won't be long now."

"Well, if they're thinking about moving, it could be a few minutes before they move," says Seb. "Sometimes it can take humans a while to think things through."

I laugh at Seb's funny remark and continue to do so for several seconds. Gemma scowls at me and puts her paw on my mouth to show I should stop.

"It was not that funny, Frederick," she says, and we trot off towards the tree, followed by the crows and Oliver. Rufus heads over towards the slide to await his moment.

"The council people are getting out of their vehicle," says Ron. I glance around and discover there are three people, two women and a man, stretching their legs and slowly heading towards the tree.

The people with cameras head towards us too and it seems like the tree and we animals are surrounded.

The people from the parks board are about five yards from the tree when Oliver jumps into the tree and faces the approaching humans. Gemma and I join him and put our paws around Oliver's shoulders in a show of solidarity. The crows jump onto the branches as do six sparrows and four finches. Starlings gather in the branches above.

There are seven cameras pointing at us.

"Well, I never expected this," says the first lady as she rubs her ginger hair with slight exasperation. "We can't remove the tree with the local wildlife in it."

"We could scare them away," says the man with a bald head and glasses.

"How would that work in front of all these cameras?" says the second lady. "You can imagine the headlines, Tony. Park employees attack wildlife."

"I can, Betty. That calico cat is giving me a nasty sneer. I bet she'd scratch me if I came any closer."

"What shall we do?" asks the first lady. "I know. I'll get closer and find out how the animals react. They might just run away of their own accord."

With that, she moves closer to us and Gemma glares at her, gauging the distance to determine whether she can swipe a paw at her while remaining in the tree – it's a question of not overbalancing. The lady comes closer, and the crows start to caw and flap their wings. Gemma takes a swipe just to measure the distance but misses by about six inches. The lady stops.

"They're not running off, are they?" says Tony.

"They're not, Tony. We might have to come back at a different time and reassess the situation and hopefully there won't be as many cameras here. It's almost as though there was a social media campaign to get some publicity for this animal protest. I've never seen cats, crows, and other birds unite in this manner. I'll have to ask an animal behaviourist, as it seems like they're all cooperating together."

The three council people back away slowly. Cameramen pointing their cameras at us quickly replaced them. Gemma loses her sneer and looks straight at the cameras.

"Can someone tell Rufus to slide?" I say.

"He's just starting," says Stan. "He's at the top of the slide right now."

The council employees return to their vehicle and Betty is on her phone.

The cameras pan around from the council vehicle to the tree and then one reporter points towards the slide and four of the cameramen head over there straight away.

"How long should we stay here?" asks Oliver.

"Until the council people have driven off and left the park," I say, "we can't take any chances. They might return now that some cameramen have left the tree."

"There are seven members of the public in attendance too, so I doubt the council will do anything with them there," says Reg. "I'm not sure who they are, but they're definitely interested in what we're doing."

"Rufus seems to be jumping well," says Andrea, "and the cameras are loving him."

"Here's Penny and her little dog," I say. "She's on our side."

"Well done, Freddie and Gemma," says Penny, "you should be proud of what you've done."

"Don't sneer at her, Gemma," I say. "She's with us."

"It's because of her John combed me severely and pulled my fur," says Gemma, "but you're right, there's more important things at stake here, so I will remove the sneer."

Gemma miaows at Penny, and I join in.

Penny turns to the people around the tree. "These cats and birds are environmentalists. The council was going to chop the tree down."

"Good for them," says one man, "the council should leave the tree alone 'cos the wasps aren't here any longer."

"Will the council come back?" says a woman.

"They might," says another, "but knowing their bureaucrat ways, they'll have to pin a communication on the tree first, so people have time to object."

This is an interesting point for me, as I understood the council were just advertising their deeds. I hadn't realised it was so humans could object. At that moment, the vehicle containing the council employees drives off. Some humans seem to wave them 'au revoir'. The vehicle is trailing a large metallic machine I presume would cut up the tree into small pieces called biomass, which would burn to produce heat. This is counterproductive, as this process would release carbon dioxide into the atmosphere and stop excess heat from leaving the surface of the earth, our Earth.

As the council employees have gone, we have to decide how to make sure we find out when the council will come to inspect the tree again.

"How many days' notice do they give?" asks Oliver.

"The last one was seventy-two hours ahead," says Stan.

"We have to check every day and regroup at the right time," says Gemma, "because they will try again, and we have to stop them."

"I can't wait to watch the news," I say. "It will help our campaign if we come across well on the TV. The council might not be so keen to desecrate the tree if there are people in attendance."

"That's true," says Rob, "we should all head down to the slide and be seen supporting our flying squirrel friend who is entertaining the cameras."

"We'll perch on the side of the slide," says Ethel, a finch with green on her wingtips, "and encourage Rufus as he flies by."

"Great idea, Ethel," says Ron. "We'll join you and caw as he goes past."

We vacate the tree and head over to Rufus, who is doing well with his flying. He pretends not to be aware of the cameras while showing off just a little. The birds sit on the slide and make a noise as he goes past. He's worked out how to do a somersault now and lands on his feet most of the time. The cameramen and reporters are all smiling.

"You should have a go, Freddie," says Ron. "A cat or two going on the slide would be memorable."

"You're right," I say, "let's have a go, Gemma and Iver."

I climb the steps and compose myself before heading down the slide tail first with my feet in the air. I correct myself before I rotate too much and land on my paws, as cats are supposed to do. A reporter puts a microphone in front of me and I give a long miaow and stare into the camera.

"You are such a photogenic kitty cat," says the reporter, "and this is amazing TV. I can't believe this is happening."

Oliver tries too hard to do a somersault and doesn't quite make it, landing on his front paws quite hard, but he is okay.

Gemma climbs up the steps and goes down paws first. She stops at the bottom of the slide before jumping off the end. All the humans laugh aloud, and Gemma waves at the cameras with her right paw.

"Brilliant, Gemma," says Stan, "I reckon that will be on TV."

"I wonder where that came from?" says Gemma. "I was trying my best to slide off the end, but I just came to a halt. What else could I do but jump off? Rufus would have knocked me over otherwise."

"I like the wave," I tell her. "It was regal."

"Thank you," says Gemma. "We should stop now, leave them wanting more."

"Good idea," I say. "Rufus, perhaps we should leave some flying for the next time we're entertaining the TV people."

"I quite agree. You can have too much of a good thing," says Rufus. "Will I be on TV?"

"Definitely," I reply, "we'll try to record it, so we can show you. Gemma is going to use the remote control to record the local news this evening. Our humans normally watch it, and their reaction will be interesting."

"Will they be upset with you?" says Rufus.

"They'll be concerned that we crossed a road to get to the park, because they care what happens to Gemma and me, especially when they're out of the house. They might close the window so we can't get out. Though I reckon they know we go out and about when they're at work, but seeing the film will reinforce this understanding and they might not be too happy with us."

"They'll be pleased you're getting involved in environmental issues," says Rufus. "You'll see, it really adds publicity to a cause, and that's what environmental groups want."

"Rufus, you know more about this than I do," I reply, "but you're correct. I hope people remember that the council wants to chop a tree down rather than remembering animals sitting in a tree and playing on a slide."

"Well, that depends on the reporter's angle," says Rob. "They'll show people the tree, and the council's written communication, and the council employees, so that the viewers will understand the idea."

"True, Rob, true," says Gemma, "anyway we should get back. I have to confirm I know how to program the recorder using the remote this afternoon, so I should start as soon as I can. We'll show you the recording tomorrow if I work it out, of course."

"I'm sure you will," says Stan. "You work things out quickly."

"I will do my best," replies Gemma. "There are many buttons on the remotes and sometimes I believe they were designed for an octopus to use, not a human."

The crows and finches find this amusing and caw and tweet their appreciation. We agree to meet at the same time tomorrow morning to discover what notice the council places on the tree, letting the humans know when the council will try again to evaluate the tree. Rob confirms that Aubrey and Arabella will be visiting on the next day, probably in the afternoon. It seems like everything is falling into place, although what picture will be made, I'm not sure yet. Oliver says au revoir and heads back to his house. Two reporters follow him out of the park and make a note of his address.

Rufus, Gemma, and I head back towards the road. I glance back occasionally to find out whether we're being observed. At the top of the grassy bank, we try to discover whether the man we spied earlier is still in his car. Although the car is no longer in the same place, Rufus spots that he's moved the car to the other side of the road, where he can still view the house. I look behind me again.

"Three reporters are watching us," I say, "like they did with Oliver. They're noting where we go, so there might well be a knock on the door later when our human parents come home from work."

"Well," says Gemma, smiling at me, "it's out of our hands now. In a few days, people's attention will be elsewhere, so let's enjoy the feeling of being important while it lasts."

"It will last longer than that," says Rufus, "and I'd like to know who that man in the car works for. He must work for the security forces. Anyway, let's get across the road safely and securely, otherwise all this talk of the future will be irrelevant."

"Excellent point," says Gemma. "Thank you for saying that, Rufus. Let's get to the other side of the road and then take it from there."

We let two vehicles pass before trotting across the road. Rufus wishes us a good day and heads up his tree. I decide to talk to Holly whilst Gemma heads indoors to program the remote control. She seems motivated and full of resolve, as though she has found another vocation in life, apart from spying.

"Hello, Holly," I say, as I jump onto her white window ledge, "how are you?"

Holly's cage sparkles in the daylight. Her human parents have polished it so well that I can discern my reflection in the bars. The straw in the bottom looks fresh.

"Freddie, you're back. I'm fine, how are you? Did anything exciting happen when you were away?" replies Holly.

"I'm fine, thank you for asking," I say. "I had some adventures in Amsterdam and had to climb down a drainpipe at one point and I survived three assassination attempts by large dogs, thanks mostly to ducking in time, persuasive argument, and a cyclist running over the dog's paw."

"Assassination? That doesn't sound too good. Are you sure you're going to be okay in your home?"

"Well, I hope so. We certainly won't be letting any large dogs into the house."

Holly had stopped running in her wheel when she started talking to me. She now looks over my shoulder.

"There's two people making a note of your address," she says. "They're under Rufus's tree."

I turn around and recognise the humans as reporters from the park. I explain what happened earlier.

"There's too many people chopping trees down," says

Holly, "all over the world. We have to stop, so I'm pleased you're doing something about this. You and Gemma and the crows are taking a stand, and this will generate a lot of publicity. Unfortunately, your humans will find out about this, and you can't know how they'll react."

"My human parents will be happy we're trying to preserve trees but concerned that we're crossing a road to do so," I say, "but they'll understand and support us in any way they can. I doubt they'll close all the windows and stop us from leaving the house."

"Yes, that's the danger, isn't it, that they overreact and leave you as prisoners in the house during the day? They seem kind though, so I don't think they'll do that."

"How are you, Holly?" I ask. "Are you running as much as a few weeks ago?"

"I'm cutting down slightly," replies Holly, "and when I run, I'm not going as quickly as I can't see the point. I'm looking out of the window more and observing things. Such as the man who was sitting outside your house when you were away. I first noticed him two days after you left, and he only seemed to be here when your cat sitter wasn't. It was almost as though he was a house sitter if you like."

"That's interesting," I say, "so he's on our side then? Was he around in the evening? Could you tell?"

"I couldn't tell, but your cat sitter was here every evening without fail, and the lights were on in at least one room. She also moved the two cat toys around each day, so you were never in the same place on consecutive days, a bit like actual cats, of course."

I miaow with happiness at this witticism. It's true, cats are always seeking new vantage points to contemplate their surroundings.

"What's Gemma doing now?" asks Holly.

"She's expecting that our environmentalist stance will be on the local news this evening and is programming the recording machine connected to the TV so that we can watch it again and show the other animals how the news was reported. She's quite proud about how we all stuck together. It's a pity your cage wasn't open, otherwise you could have come too."

"Well, when the council people come back to the park next time, perhaps I can come over with you then? I doubt my human parents would recognise me on the television."

"We'll definitely check your window to discover which way you're running," I reassure her. "The more animals we can muster, the better."

"And the more newsworthy it will be," says Holly, "hopefully this can be the start of something."

"I really do hope so," I reply. "It's our planet too and the humans forget that. Some of them are very selfish and want to take everything just for themselves so they can make more money. All most of us want is to feel safe and appreciated."

"That's right, you should be a politician. You put your point across well."

"Thank you. It's nice to be appreciated. Don't forget you're invited over when we get the chance to read some books on Egypt. Our humans will have to borrow the books first, of course. I will have to organise that part by planting a big hint next to their library cards."

"I'd prefer to attend the protest, in preference to reading a book, though I suppose we could do both. Make a day of it if you like?"

"Sounds like a great idea. I'll have to put that guidebook to Egypt under John's library card, so he gets the hint. Though he might ignore it, especially in the morning. How are your human parents? They are still interested in gardening, by the looks of it."

As I say this, I look at the garden with its neatly trimmed lawn and flower beds with each individual leaf of every plant clearly visible, without the hint of a weed.

"They're still interested in gardening – most of the wasps have gone by the sounds of it, presumably because you persuaded them to move a few weeks ago to another nest further away. They're talking of bringing me outside in the garden when it's a nice day, so I can get some fresh air. I'm looking forward to that. My human parents are going to create a fragrance garden in my honour, and I might even run around outside the cage, they say."

"That sounds like something to look forward to," I say. "You're lucky your parents think about your welfare. I wonder what fragrances they'll put in a fragrance garden. Lavender presumably and Lilies and Phloxes."

"Yes, that's right, and Lily of the Valley and Peonies. That's all they mentioned."

"It will smell nice," I say, "and will attract bees too, which has to be a good thing. The more pollinators, the better."

As if to emphasise the point, a bumblebee comes to say hello and buzzes around my head twice before heading off towards a patch of clover in our garden. My human parents don't work too hard in our garden and so it has a more natural appearance, a bit overrun in places, but the plants seem to enjoy themselves and are keen to spread out as much as they can.

"Do you speak bumblebee?" asks Holly.

"I didn't think so," I say, "but I reckon insects pick up on the tone of sounds, especially the positive sounds."

"Wavelengths, they're on the same wavelength as you and tune into your positive feelings."

I stare at the bricks of the chimney as it soars into the blue sky for a few seconds. I'm still a little embarrassed when given compliments and start blushing.

"Thank you. That's nice of you to say so."

"I should get a bit of exercise now," says Holly. "I'll go for a quick sprint and then have a nap."

"That sounds like a good idea," I reply. "I'm going to run around your fence a few times to get some exercise too, before eating a snack. Take care, Holly. I'll speak to you soon."

With that, I jump onto the fence and sort my paws out before building up a pleasant rhythm as I trot around the fence. Holly's human parents seem to have painted some panels a light-blue colour while others are white, which makes for a colourful setting. I try not to step on the places where the white and blue colours meet. I believe it will bring me bad luck, like stepping on the gaps between paving stones.

Now, I'm not sure why I think that, but I do, which is why a disciplined trotting technique is required to make sure no bad luck comes my way. It's good practice to have the correct posture when moving along as it preserves your skeleton and stops you from getting aches and pains. At least that's what I read in a fitness magazine that Mary bought a few weeks ago. I also read about the correct technique for doing bicep curls, but I'm not sure whether cats possess biceps and even if we do, I'm not sure whether I could grip the weight properly. The weights in the photo of the smiling model with beautiful white teeth seemed smooth to me and designed for human fingers. My paws aren't as large and flexible as a human hand, so I'd have to find another method to do this exercise.

Luckily, my paws can grip the trellis that the Lancashire Rose is climbing, and I haul myself upwards with success. I climb in through the window and hear the television. I walk through to the Lounge to find Gemma is watching a program.

"What is on the TV?" I ask.

"It's a recording, Frederick. I've sorted out the remote gizmo, and so I programmed the TV to record this drivel about angst-ridden people blurting out their fears on live TV. There we are. It's stopped now. So, I'll just press the delete button for that recording and set the recording for 6pm to 7pm on Channel 1, as that will include local news at some point."

"We should check the list of TV channels, because the vans I made a mental note of were for small local TV stations, so we have a better chance of appearing on those channels."

"Oh, good idea, there's a list function here," says Gemma,

peering at the instructions. "Et voila, are any of those familiar?" She showed me the list.

"Yes, numbers twenty-two, thirty-five, and thirty-six Gemma. They all had cameras and reporters in the park just now."

"These TV remote controls weren't designed for cats to use," says Gemma, fiddling with some buttons, "I'll try to record Channel 22 news now when is it on… Oh, 6pm so let me try to press the little arrow… Oh, wrong way… There we are all set; I'll try to do the same for Channel 35 and Channel 36."

"I'm amazed at how quickly you pick these things up, Gemma. You're dexterous and patient."

"Thank you, but I have a vested interest, because I want to look at myself on TV glaring at that council official, and I want to see us in the tree, looking after the natural world. Showing the humans how to protest effectively, that it's deeds that count not words and that your actions define who you are. I hope some humans will come and help us next time. If we can get the council to preserve the tree, this will show that peaceful protests can be effective and will encourage others to do the same."

"That is true," I reply. "We should set an example and hopefully our human friends can help us preserve trees and nature."

"What will be interesting," says Gemma, narrowing her eyes slightly, "is whether our humans will spot us on the news directly or whether they'll only find out when their friend Penny rings them up and the reporters knock on the front door, which they will do. They might be confused for a while. Should we hang around or make ourselves scarce?"

"We should be here," I say. "We should be available to show that we've nothing to hide and nothing to be ashamed of. They'll only be upset with us for crossing the road, which they regard as dangerous for cats."

"Right," says Gemma. "They won't be completely upset with us, but they'll have to be nice about us with the reporters that come and with any friends that ring them up. Most of the contact will probably be via social media, so we won't be aware of it, other than hearing all their notifications, those pings, dings, and rings that punctuate their evenings, the commas, full stops, and quotation marks of silence."

"That's poetic," I say. "Lots of rhyming in that sentence."

"Thank you," replies Gemma. "I'll have to start writing down my ideas. Which reminds me, I must start that murder / mystery story I had an idea about on the train to Amsterdam involving the pet shop owner whose animals go and solve local mysteries when he's asleep, which is most of the time. Anyway, I'll have a nap, but I will set the alarm for 5:50pm to make sure I'm awake in time to come upstairs. I want to find out our humans' reaction to the protest. This is going to be amusing."

With this bon mot, she trots downstairs, leaving me to read my latest book by Joseph Campbell about the Arthurian Romances and in particular the work *Parzival* by Wolfram von Eschenbach. Joseph gives an excellent commentary on this epic poem written at the beginning of the 13th Century about the adventures of Parzival and Gawain in their quest for the Holy Grail. It's quite enthralling even though there are no cats in the story, but there are lots of contests between Parzival and other knights, all of whom he defeats and sends off to Camelot and the court of King Arthur. He meets lots of maidens on the way to the Grail Castle, which he enters for a second time and heals the wound of Anfortas, the Fisher King, by asking a simple question.

I fall asleep and have a dream about a knight who wears red armour defending a tree against attack by people wearing high-resolution vests. The knight purrs when he / she scares off the people by prodding them with a lance.

I wake up as John comes through the front door. He puts a burrito in the microwave and goes downstairs to put out our dinner and clean the litter trays. He comes back upstairs, closely followed by Gemma, who jumps onto the couch.

"Are you kitties alright?" he asks. "I've just put your food out and you normally zoom downstairs and start eating."

Gemma stares at the TV and I miaow to indicate I'm fine where I am.

John gets his burrito and slices it into equal size pieces before switching on the television and sitting down on the couch, moving a yellow cushion, so that he doesn't sit directly on it. Channel 22 is on, and the headlines are being read out. I hear the tail end of something that sounds like "...and an unusual protest in a local park sparks interest, especially when a squirrel starts using a slide... more later."

"What?" says John. "That looked like the park over the road."

He starts eating his food but doesn't switch channels.

A few minutes later, Mary comes in, having cooked herself some pasta in a vegetable sauce.

"Why are you watching this channel?" she asks. "We never watch this channel."

"It was the channel that was on when I switched on the TV."

"How can that be? We never watch this channel."

"It mentioned a protest in a park, and it was the park over the road, so I'd like to find out who was protesting. When I went for a run this morning, there was no one around."

Gemma is sitting on the back of the couch, doing her best to look aloof. I sit on the arm of the chair and watch the TV. After about fifteen minutes, following a story about a parrot who escaped from its home and had to be rescued from a tall tree, the announcer says: "And now for a really heart-warming story about some animals who occupied a tree to stop it being chopped down by the local council." Then the pictures start.

Gemma cranes forward, and I stare at the screen.

"That is the local park," says John. "That's the tree where the wasps' nest was before they left to go somewhere else."

"Oh my," says Mary, "look at those cats in the tree with the crows..." her voice trails off as she has suddenly realised something.

"Wait, that's... wait, this is being recorded," says John. "Did you set this to record on this channel 22?"

"No," says Mary, "we don't watch Channel 22, John, so why would I record a channel that we never watch?"

"But who set this to record then?" says John, looking at

Gemma, who avoids his stare with ease as she's still looking at the pictures on the screen. Her tail is wagging.

"Right, because it's being recorded, we can go back two or three minutes and stop the recording at certain places where certain characters can be seen."

John presses the rewind button, and we relive recent history in reverse at high speed. He stops rewind, and the recording proceeds at normal speed. Gemma's glare is clear for all to admire. My smile at the camera looks nice. The crows are noisy, far noisier than I realised at the time. John and Mary glance at each other. There's a knock at the door.

"I wonder who that is?" asks Mary. "And I wonder if it's related to our tree-hugging kitties here?" She smiles and looks at me with a certain combination of admiration and worry.

"Let's find out, shall we?" says John, looking at me rather ruefully.

John opens the door and there's someone there he's never met before.

"Can I help you?" he asks.

"Yes, are you the owner of two of the cats who took part in a protest in the park earlier today?" says a female voice.

"Yes, I am, well, we are. Both of us are." John gestures towards Mary. "We've only just found out about their protest on the news."

"Was that on Channel 22?" asks the reporter.

"It was, yes, was it on other channels too?" says John in disbelief.

"It was on all the channels and will be on the BBC Local

News, ITN, and Channel 4. Do you know anything about the squirrel?"

John looks at Mary with consternation – "What squirrel would that be?" asks Mary, who moves closer to the door.

"Oh, the squirrel wasn't part of the protest, but it was playing on the slide and flying off the end quite a long way... well for a squirrel anyway... and then the cats had a go too."

"I'll bet they did," says John, smiling at Gemma.

"Are the cats there? Could we have a picture?"

Gemma looks at me with something approaching trepidation.

"What do we do?" she asks. "Should we make a bolt for it? We shouldn't be seen with John and Mary. We don't want any of the bad people in the Netherlands to see our humans and discover where they live."

"We should be photographed on our own," I say.

I miaow and scoot out of the front door. Gemma sprints after me, before John and Mary can pick us up in their arms. We sit on the front steps and the reporter takes a picture of us.

"Do you know the squirrel on the slide?" she asks us.

We miaow in unison because we do know the squirrel on the slide, and we run away from the house towards Rufus's tree at the front.

At the base of the trunk, I call out: "Rufus, do you want the reporters to take your picture?"

By way of an answer, Rufus runs down the tree and blinks at the reporter before coming and standing next to us. He stares at the camera as the snaps are taken by the reporter who is almost kneeling on the ground – she must have strong thighs.

"Oh, squirrel," says the reporter, "I wish you could tell us how long you've been using the slide for."

"How long have you been flying for?" I ask Rufus.

"It's about eight months now," replies Rufus, "give or take a week or two."

I miaow eight times to the reporter, who looks at me in a confused manner: "Does eight miaows mean eight days, or eight weeks, or eight months, kitty?"

Gemma miaows three times to indicate the third choice, i.e. eight months.

"Eight months?" says the reporter.

Gemma miaows once to indicate 'Yes'.

"Right," says the reporter, turning to Mary and John, "your kitties seem to understand English. Is that possible?"

"I don't understand how they could," says Mary. "How would they have done that?"

"Animal intuition?" says the reporter, "who knows, but I reckon your male cat asked the squirrel something and the squirrel replied and then he miaowed eight times to me, so there's some form of intelligent communication taking place. Anyway, I'm impressed at their environmentalist approach, and I hope you don't mind if we use their photos online and in the paper?"

"Yes, that's fine," says John.

"And what about a picture of yourselves?"

Gemma approaches the reporter, who is still kneeling down and puts her right-front paw on the camera and then looks at Mary and John in an almost pleading way.

"Looks like Gemma doesn't want us to be photographed,"

says Mary, "and that's probably a good thing as we aren't the story here are we, it's the cats and the animals that are the story, so Gemma is right to indicate that."

"Well done," I say.

"I don't want them getting hurt by those nasty people we were following in Amsterdam," she replies. "It's not their fault."

"That's caring of you," I reply.

"What's she referring to?" asks Rufus, still staring at the reporter.

"It's regarding our time away, Rufus," I reply. "We were helping some people keep track of some other people who were breaking the law or suspected of breaking the law."

"Well, that sounds dangerous to me," says Rufus, "so I hope you're all going to be okay. When can I see myself jumping off the slide?"

"We didn't get that far," says Gemma. "The reporter knocked on the door before the part about the slide, but we'll check tomorrow morning and tell you straight away what we find. I'll also find the pictures the reporter just took of you and show you those."

"Thank you," says Rufus. "That sounds good to me."

The reporter stands up and smiles at John and Mary: "You'll be getting lots of visitors wanting to meet those kitties of yours and they'll probably be asked to open summer fetes and take part in other environmental activities – I hope you're ready for that." With that, she thanked us all for our time and walked over the road towards the park.

"We'll get plenty of visitors, will we?" says Gemma. "I'm

not sure that'll be a good thing. I hope John and Mary don't close the window so we can't get out."

"They might do, because they'll be trying to protect us from ourselves rather than from other people," I reply. "Primarily, they'll be concerned we're crossing the road unsupervised rather than us being in the media spotlight."

"Yes," says Gemma, "but I'm of the opposite opinion. I'm not keen for us to be in the media spotlight. John and Mary aren't aware we've been away, are they?"

"We can't tell them, can we?" I reply.

"Perhaps they'll find out from social media?" says Rufus. "That's how most humans find out about things, isn't it?"

"That's true," says Gemma. "You may well be right, Rufus."

John and Mary start to head indoors, and we indicate to Rufus we should follow them. He smiles, wishes us a pleasant evening, and looks forward to seeing the video tomorrow.

When we get inside, John strokes us both and says he hopes we take care when crossing the road. Mary nods and gives us both a kiss on the top of the head.

Gemma looks mortified and jumps onto the back of the couch where I join her.

"Well, Freddie and Gemma, let's play the whole of that report on Channel 22, because there's more to come," says John.

Sure enough, Channel 22 did make a great deal of the protest as well as the slide where both my jump and Gemma's leap off the end of the slide are recorded. Rufus took pride of place with three of his jumps featured, including a perfect somersault which would surely have won a gold medal at the squirrel Olympics.

"The things these animals get up to when we're at work," says Mary smiling at us, "you do realise there's going to be a lot of people in the park tomorrow, expecting you to put on a show for them?"

Gemma looks at me: "She might be correct, but one of us should go over tomorrow and check the tree to find out whether another communication has been put there by the council."

"Yes, you're right. I'll go with Rufus and check. I'm sure Rufus will provide some entertainment for anyone who's there. It's a working day, so perhaps there won't be many people there?"

"We shall have to wait," says Gemma. "When you come back with Rufus, make sure you bring him to the window, so we can show him the video of his leaps. He looks impressive."

"I will," I say, and look to find out whether the news is still recording. It isn't which shows that Gemma programmed the recorder correctly.

"When Rufus mentioned social media, I thought of something else. People will have seen us on TV and they're now more likely to recognise us if we appear on social media – for example, at the airport or when I was photographed in the back of the vehicle in Amsterdam. What happens if John and Mary are sent those examples? They'll start asking questions and probably contact Mrs Elkins."

"That's out of our control, isn't it? We can't do anything

about that now, so you should be stoic about it. We'll be seeing Aub and Arabella tomorrow, don't forget, and perhaps they can reassure us about what's likely to happen next."

Gemma stretches along the back of the couch and looks at me.

"You're right, I should remember what I read. I'm going to have a little nap and meditate to see if that helps." She tucks her feet under her, in what I call the loaf of bread position, and stares at the wall.

I jump under the couch where I've carefully stowed Joseph Campbell. I start to read as John and Mary watch the television, although when I look up, they're watching the recording of the tree protest and the antics of Rufus.

The book is learned, authoritative, and riveting to read as Campbell brings together myths from Wales, Ireland, the European continent, the Middle East, and even further afield to support the explanation of the tales featured in the book.

The book starts with explanations of the Neolithic, Celtic, Roman, and German backgrounds for the myths. Then the voyages of St Brendan are explained and the life of St Patrick, as well as the roles of troubadours and Minnesingers in the Middle Ages.

There are in-depth studies of Wolfram von Eschenbach's Parzival, Gottfried von Strassburg's Tristan and Iseult and the Knights of the Round Table as well as good analysis of the Waste Land, The Fisher King, The Grail, and Avalon.

Once again, these stories seem to have a common source which has now been lost, and that's a great shame unless, of course, the common source was an oral tale passed down over the centuries as most humans couldn't read and write. An oral source would also explain how these stories were found over most of the European continent as travelling storytellers would spread the tales over long distances quite quickly. This is something that cats don't seem to have, as my mum didn't tell me stories about the exploits of our ancestors. I know we wouldn't have ridden around on horses looking for castles containing holy cups and chalices, but we might have done something interesting like looking for wonderful fish in shady ponds or climbing three-hundred-feet high trees in search of colourful birds with exotic plumage.

I'm pleased to say John and Mary don't delete the recording from Channel 22, so we can show the report to Rufus and the crows tomorrow, assuming they can all perch on the window ledge in a safe manner. I think the finches and sparrows would want to see themselves on human TV too, so it could get a bit crowded. It will be a busy day tomorrow as Aub and Arabella will be coming and debriefing us on our trip to Amsterdam.

I fall asleep and dream about riding around on a small horse, stopping at massive castles and drinking water from a saucer placed outside near the drawbridge. A hosepipe hangs down from above and drips water into the saucer so that it's always being replenished for thirsty travelling felines such as myself, Sir Freddie Cat, or, as Gemma might call me, Sir Frederick.

Chapter 5

Today

I WAKE UP. MY TONGUE is lolling out of my mouth. It's because of the dream I was having before waking. In my dream, I was licking up a bowl of liquid outside a castle called Mouselvache when a fair damsel with golden hair comes running out of the castle saying that I, Sir Freddie Cat, am the chosen knight to rid the castle of two evil presences, a large mouse called The Mouse and a cow originally from the pastures of The Pyrenees called El Vache. Well, what can I do? I park my horse, though I have trouble putting it into reverse, so it fits into the space available and then I scoot across the drawbridge. The damsel asks me where my lance is and I say I don't have one, but I do possess many mini lances, called claws, which come in useful on occasions such as this.

The damsel leads me down a dark passage lit only by torches at intervals of ten yards and then points upwards towards a tall tower, whose turret is lost in the misty swirls of time.

"They're up there," she shrieks and backs away, slowly, with her arms trying to block the sight of the tower. I am left alone.

"Is there a lift?" I ask, but my question reverberates around the wet stones of the walls and remains hanging in the air, cold, unanswered, and unappreciated.

There isn't a lift, but in dreams there's no harm in asking. I scamper up the stairs thanks to the magic potion in the saucer near the drawbridge and am soon above the clouds. The fog fills the passageways and then a booming sound echoes around me, followed by a squeak and a moo. The booming sound is terrifying, but the squeak and the moo are not.

I, Sir Freddie Cat, operate by stealth. I scoot down the passage and scuttle up a short flight of stairs to find a large open room, full of straw and grain, with a massive loudhailer in one corner. The mouse is measuring grain, and the cow is chewing a bale of fresh grass delivered by catapult from below.

I scrape my claws on the stone to sharpen them. The mouse and the cow are engrossed in their tasks. I scamper over to the loudhailer, turn it noiselessly in their direction, and draw a deep breath.

"MMMMMMMMMMMMMMMMMIAAAAAAAAAOOOOOOOOOOOOOOOOOOOOOOOOOOOWWWWW" I say.

Well, as if by magic, the mouse and the cow head out of the room, closely pursued by myself. We head along the passages, down the stairs, along more passages, and out over the drawbridge. The mouse and the cow don't stop, but I do because a traffic warden is placing a parking fine on my horse. Apparently, the horse is on a double-yellow line. Luckily, the golden-haired damsel pays the fine, by way of thanks, and I head off to my next adventure, but not before having a drink from the saucer, which is when I wake up.

After such an exciting start to the day, having a poo and eating my breakfast seem quite tame by comparison. By the time I arrive, Gemma has been and gone again and is doing her stretching exercises in the corridor. On my way downstairs, I observe the kitchen window remains open. This is a good thing.

I go upstairs and head under the couch and try to remain unobtrusive as John and Mary go about their morning routine. Gemma is probably staying downstairs for the same reason.

I begin a work of fiction called *Sick Heart River* by John Buchan about a dying man called Edward Leithen who goes searching for another man who's gone missing in North-Western Canada. Edward is a successful man in human terms, but he has tuberculosis and needs a last adventure to keep his spirits up. He doesn't want to go gentle into that good night and is raging against the dying of the light in his own style. In my opinion, that's all we can ever do, as life is a precious commodity.

Just before he leaves, John seeks me out and tells me to take care crossing the road today. I purr and close my eyes and open them again to show I understand. Five minutes later, Mary does the same thing, and I appreciate this gesture, too. It means they're going to leave the window open, and that's a good thing for Gemma and myself.

Once my human parents have left, I find Gemma. She is downstairs reading a book on Stoic philosophy.

"I'm going over to the park," I say. "I'll come and get you when Aubrey and Arabella arrive. You have some concerns I'm sure that you want to express to them?"

"Yes, I do. I want to find out who the person was outside the house and whether the people we were following in Amsterdam know where we live or whether they could find out because of that dratted kingfisher."

"Yes, we should find that out. Perhaps there are some records somewhere we're not aware of?"

"I'm not sure, because only Mrs Elkins knew where we lived and she left us in Brussels on the way out and no one could have followed us home, unless there was a tracking device on one of our carriers. But she took them with her when she left, so that makes little sense."

"Let's see what they tell us," I say. "We might be worrying about nothing. The man in the car was probably house watching and I've not seen any strangers around other than the reporters."

"Yes, you're probably right. I'll stop worrying and read some more Epictetus. Take care when crossing the road. John and Mary are worried about you."

"Another thing you could do," I reply, "is that you could start planning your mystery book, where the pets in the pet shop solve crimes and that would use your creativity which is currently being used for worrying about events and anticipating them."

"Oh, what a great idea, yes, I could plan that. Now the humans have gone to work, I can access the folder on the laptop and write the characters' names and what their

~ 73 ~

individual strengths are. And work out what crimes will need solving. And how they'll get in and out of the pet shop without the owner knowing what they're doing. I'll do that now, thank you."

"I will catch you later," I reply and head upstairs. The window is open the same amount as normal. I wish a cheery 'Good Morning' to the plants on the counter and to the Lancashire Rose as I climb down to the lawn.

Rob is walking around the lawn looking for grubs for himself and his family. He wishes me a hearty 'Good morning, Freddie' and I reply in kind.

"Are you aware of a new communication on the tree?" I ask. Crows are observant and discover things well before most other creatures of my acquaintance.

"There was some activity around the tree this morning," says Rob, "but I can't be sure who it was. Council people usually wear those high-visibility vests, and none of the people had those jackets on. Perhaps they were tourists looking for the tree from the news?"

"That could well be true," I reply. "We'll show you the news report when we come back from the park. All the family were on film."

"That's good to hear," says Rob. "What did your humans say?"

"They're mainly concerned about us crossing the road," I reply, "and us being safe. As long as we're careful, I'm not sure they mind too much."

"You're lucky to have such considerate humans, Freddie. A lot of them don't let their cats out of the house or they throw them outside when it's raining and let the poor cat find somewhere dry."

"Yes, I've heard stories like that from other cats at the cat shelter where I lived. I'm lucky to have found such wonderful humans to live with."

"Oh, I should just confirm with you that Aubrey and Arabella will now be here later this morning."

"That's good," I say. "Gemma will be interested in what they have to say. She's eager to find out who the man was watching the house when we were away."

"We'd all like to know, though to be fair he never once came up to the house. He always stayed in the car."

"Well, I hope we find out later this morning. Anyway, I'm going over to the park to discover what's going on with that tree. Are you coming over?"

"Oh yes, I'll be over when I've finished my breakfast. I just need another two worms, Freddie. I shan't be long."

I smile and trot over to the tree in the front garden where I wait for Rufus to come down the trunk, so we can head over to the park together.

"Hello, Freddie," says my squirrel friend as he heads downwards at a rapid rate, "I'm pleased your humans let you out of the house. I was worried they wouldn't."

"You and me both," I reply, "and Gemma was worried too. Today, many people will come to see you perform on the slide."

"Yes, there's some people over there already from what I could see from my drey, but it'll be okay as long as they don't get in the way."

"Well, humans get in the way, though it's mainly from enthusiasm rather than malicious intent."

We're sitting on the roots of the tree and there seem to be more cars than usual parked alongside the road. On the opposite side, some people are walking along the footpath and pointing towards the park with their umbrellas as the forecast is for rain.

"We should be careful crossing," says Rufus, "as there are fewer places than usual to get a good view. We'll have to sneak out between two cars. Unless the crows can help us, they are over there."

"Jacqueline is flying over here," I say. "Perhaps she can help?"

"Hello, Rufus and Freddie," says the female crow, "there are quite a few humans over there in the park already. Do you want me to caw when the road's clear?"

"That would be great," I say.

Jacqueline jumps onto the top of a blue car and looks up and down the road. Rufus and I wait patiently by the side of the road until Jacqueline starts her raucous calling. We still both check each way before running across the road and up the grassy bank.

Jacqueline lands close by, as do Andrea and Seb.

"Good morning, Andrea and Seb," I say. "How are you?"

"I'm fine, thank you," says Andrea, "young Oliver is sitting in the tree already having his photo taken."

"Yes, morning, Freddie and Rufus, there's a new notice on the tree," says Seb, "and the council will be returning on Saturday to re-evaluate the tree situation."

"Saturday?" I say. "Oh, that's not good. The humans are at home on Saturdays, and we don't normally go out."

"They'll have to make an exception, won't they?" says Rufus. "We'll come and knock on the door and ask if you can come out to play."

"Thank you," I say as the crows caw with mirth.

There are a dozen people looking at the tree, with Oliver sitting on one branch. Over at the playground, some children are playing on the slide and swings as their parents look on.

"We should say hello to Iver," I say. "He looks a bit isolated in that tree. He needs our support." With that, I scurry off towards Oliver. Rufus scampers after me and the crows fly on ahead.

"Hello, Freddie," says Oliver, "have you seen the notice on the trunk of the tree?"

"I've seen it. I'll just clamber up and read it," I reply.

I check my claws to make sure they're all in good condition and clamber up the bark to get closer to the white piece of paper covered in plastic to protect the information against the rain that will almost certainly fall between now and Saturday at 10am which is when the council will return. In some ways, this isn't as important as Martin Luther attaching ninety-five theses to the door of the Castle Church in Wittenberg on 31st October 1517, but the next inspection could be the start of a reformation of humans' attitudes towards preserving the environment. We have to start somewhere and realise every tree is a precious commodity. Most of the humans taking pictures of me climbing the trunk are here for the novelty value, but if it makes one person ponder the situation, then it will be worth it. Our presence might be a gimmick, but the more people who are aware, the better it is.

"Hello, Iver," I say. "How long have you been here for?"

"About forty-five minutes, Freddie. The people started coming into the park about 9am, and I saw them when I was eating my breakfast, so I decided I should come over to keep the people interested. There's more over by the slide waiting for Rufus."

Rufus looks over towards the children's playground and smiles.

"Freddie, I'm going over to the slide, so the people can watch me. Are you going to come over later?"

"I'm sure we will be," I say. "We need some exercise."

Rufus smiles and flops and hops towards the playground over the grass. When he's about twenty yards away, the children point, and the parents search for their phones so they can take pictures. Such is their distraction that one swing hits an adult in the back and causes him to clutch at himself in pain. The child on the swing tries to suppress a giggle.

I clamber up by Oliver and people take pictures of us sitting on the branch. I point my front-right paw at the notice to indicate what we're protesting about.

"The cats are protesting about the tree," says one lady. "I knew they were. And here come the crows."

Sure enough, our crow friends land on the branches and caw in unison.

"Hello, Freddie and Iver," says Stan, "how are things?

Plenty of people around. It must have been on the news channels last night."

"Yes, it was on Channel 35," says Oliver. "My owners Simon and Samantha missed it at first until the male reporter knocked on the door and told them about it. They replayed it and searched on other channels. The reporter says that overseas channels in the Benelux countries were interested in the reports as they like eccentric stories from the UK about people doing strange things in odd situations."

"Oh, really?" I say. I'm not sure whether to be pleased about this or not. On the one hand, I was dyed most of the time in the Netherlands, but on the other hand, Gemma would be easily recognised.

"There was also a story about a squirrel jumping off a slide."

"Rufus would have appeared on the television in the Netherlands?"

"Yes," says Oliver, giggling, "why is the Netherlands important?"

I contemplate before replying. "I know Rufus is popular in that country. He's admired there because he keeps getting up after he lands on his face."

"Oh, good for Rufus, I suppose. Is Gemma coming over today?"

"No, Iver. She's planning her book about pets who solve crimes. She's getting all the character names sorted out, and the plot lines for the stories."

"You two keep busy, don't you?"

"We try to improve ourselves and help others whenever

we can. We're now branching out, if you'll pardon the phrase, into helping trees and the environment. Who are these two people, Iver? They seem to know you."

"That's Simon and Samantha. They're both originally from Hong Kong and they love Chinese food. They're wonderful cooks and let me lick their plates. I like Hoisin sauce; it's the fermented soybean paste I like."

"They look nice," I reply, wondering whether I could use ESP to ask Mary and John to buy some Hoisin sauce for me to sample. This would be an excellent test of my skills as an influencer via thought transfer and would replace onions as my foodstuff of choice to bring back from the supermarket on their next shopping trip.

"Hello, Oliver, who's your friend?" asks Samantha. She's tall with short black hair and glasses that have a red rim. Simon is the same height as Samantha and smiles at me, showing some extremely white teeth. I miaow at him by way of welcome.

Samantha reads the notice and turns to Simon. "The council is coming back on Saturday, so we should come out and make sure they don't cut down the tree. We should support Olly and his friend here, who are the first animal activists I've heard of."

Not wishing to be forgotten, the crows caw and kick up a fuss as they're part of the protest.

"The crows are reminding us that this is a proper protest and not just cats sitting in a tree," says Simon.

"I wonder where the other kitty is, the calico cat, who glared at the council official?" asks Samantha. I miaow again.

"She lives with you, does she?" asks Samantha.

I miaow as she is right, of course.

"We'll have to meet your owners on Saturday," says Simon to me, "as I hope they'll come to the park to support their cats."

I hope they do too. Some human help for our cause would be most welcome. I have an idea and stare at Samantha intently whilst repeating the words 'Hoisin Sauce" in my mind.

"We should bring some food for people to share," says Simon, "and make it a social occasion for people who live around the park."

I glance at Simon and wonder why my thoughts travelled at the wrong angle to him and not to Samantha, who was straight in front of me. Perhaps thoughts don't travel in straight lines but are in fact like waves in the sea and go up and down or perhaps from side to side, which would explain why Simon received my idea rather than Samantha.

"That's a lovely idea. We could knock up a large stir fry and put plenty of Hoisin sauce on it," continues Samantha. "Everyone likes Hoisin sauce, including Oliver, of course."

Now I am confused because my thoughts reached Samantha, who is nearer to me after they reached Simon, who is further away. Perhaps thought wavelengths are long and loopy, so they curved towards Simon before heading back towards Samantha. Or perhaps the thought got homesick after hitting Simon's mind and came back to me via Samantha? Or perhaps thoughts are circular and come back home to roost in my mind like chickens? This is a good puzzle for a Freddie cat to sort out on a greyish morning like today.

"We should head over to see how Rufus is getting on with entertaining the crowds down there and bring him back here, so he sits in the tree with us. That way, all the people down there will read the council's communication and come back tomorrow." Oliver's suggestion is excellent, so I jump down from the tree and scoot past the human legs with Oliver in close attendance.

Rufus is showing off to the twenty people who are watching him. He is performing a somersault on every jump from the slide and landing well. I wonder whether the squirrels in the Netherlands will still admire him, even though he no longer lands on his face. I convey Oliver's idea to him as I follow him up the steps of the slide and he says it is a great idea before plunging down the slippery, yellow slide ahead of me.

My effort is modest by comparison, but I land on my feet on the compacted grass as cats are supposed to do. Oliver takes a watching brief and we both see Rufus do two more lovely jumps before heading off towards the condemned tree. About half the people follow him and Oliver's idea works well as all these people look at the notice, because Rufus sits in the tree and points down at it. There are some murmurings of discontent and then after thinking for a few seconds, one child asks why the council is going to chop down a tree which is used by cats, squirrels, and birds as an armchair. No one has a suitable answer for the little girl and so I miaow to her, showing I appreciate her concerns for the environment. She looks at me, points, and shouts, 'Kitty spoke to me'. I have to be careful that the ESP doesn't get out of hand, otherwise I'll be taken to a university laboratory and kept there for a long period to determine what thoughts cats have daily. In that case, I'd revert to thinking about meals, sleeping, and staring out of the window. This would soon make them release me, although it would be a great opportunity to meditate and clear my mind of all thoughts. This would make the ESP researchers even more unhappy as it would be the opposite of what they'd require for good and meaningful research. They'd label me as a cat with no thoughts rather than a Buddhist cat who can meditate effectively for long periods of time. This would be dispiriting in a way, but also a compliment.

I'm shaken out of my thoughts by Oliver, who taps me on the side to indicate it's photo time for the local newspaper people who were here yesterday, too.

"Which is my better side?" asks Rufus. "I should really find out before Saturday."

"A classical pose with you clutching a nut between both front paws would be best," says Oliver. "That will reinforce your brand as a squirrel of action, as a squirrel who lives a real squirrel's life."

Oliver has been reading a lot of marketing books, but he could well be right as Rufus could get some advertising jobs as a squirrel who jumps head over heels for a certain brand of nut. Presumably, he'd be paid in nuts too and might not have room to store them all in his drey. Fame can cause problems in areas where none existed before. Nut storage could cause Rufus some headaches. Gemma and I might help him store them in a box inside the house, but Mary and John might not appreciate this.

The photographer takes some pictures as the crows, finches, and starlings all perch in the tree. The tree must be happy with all the attention it's getting from the birds and animals and must be confident it's going to survive the council's attention. Rufus sits on a branch and clutches a nut, as Oliver suggested. The photographer takes some pictures of him in silhouette against the blue sky. Rufus holds the nut a little higher, as though he's brandishing a trophy, and the camera whirrs away like an agitated insect. The excitement is almost over as it's lunchtime and Rufus is a stickler for eating his meals at the same time each day.

I jump down to the ground as I suspect Rufus wants to leave. I'm suddenly aware of the presence of Wilf, Wasps-In-Line-Flight, around two hundred of them forming a small arrow pointing at the tree.

"What's that?" asks Oliver, who has also jumped down from the tree.

"It's the wasps," I reply, "and they wish to communicate with us. Here they go."

"Greetings," says Wilf, "how are you, Mr Freddie Cat?"

"I'm fine," I reply. "How are you all?"

"We are fine. Can we help you on Saturday as we don't want the tree to be damaged? We are upset we might have caused all this by nesting in the tree and want to make amends. Some of our more militant members want to sting, but we're trying to move our image away from such hurtful tactics, so we were wondering whether we can provide some non-threatening signage for the event? Perhaps we can form an arrow in the air and point at the tree?"

"That's a great idea. How many arrows were you thinking of?" I ask.

"Four," replies Wilf, "one for each of the cardinal points of the earth's magnetic field."

"At what height?" asks Oliver.

"We reckon ten feet," replies Wilf, "so the humans can see us, but not feel threatened."

"That sounds like a good plan," I say, "and how long would the arrows be?"

"Six feet long and two feet wide, tapering to a point."

"Is that possible?" I ask.

"We've been practising," says Wilf and immediately switch to an arrow as just described, a shimmering yellow sign that would reflect the sun without dazzling the eyes.

"That is so impressive," says Rufus. "I could use them to advertise my sliding activities."

"Let's concentrate on the tree, Rufus," I say, "and then perhaps Wilf and you can talk about advertising afterwards."

"What about a fifth arrow above the tree, pointing straight down?" asks Rufus.

"Like this?" says Wilf, effecting the change effortlessly.

A miniature fork of yellow lightning appears above us.

"Breathtaking," says Oliver, "brilliant and effortless flying synchronisation."

"Thank you," says Wilf. "It's nice to be appreciated. We'll start our pointing at 9:30am on Saturday in human time. Would that be a good idea?"

"Yes, that sounds like a great idea," I reply.

"Our scouts report a great awareness of the event from the people around here. They report snippets of conversation about the tree, the animals that are involved, and the popularity of the reporting on human television. The children are looking forward to it more than the adults. Anyway, we should be on our way. See you on Saturday, Freddie cat. It's nice to have met you, Oliver, and Rufus."

With that, Wilf heads away with a sound like the beating of a hummingbird's wings, a noise I heard when watching a nature documentary from behind Mary's head.

"How did they know who I was?" asks Oliver.

"It's fame," replies Rufus, "and it will last for over fifteen minutes, so you'll be one of the lucky ones."

"Let's hope you're right about the luck," I reply. "Being recognised is not necessarily a good thing, especially if someone or something wants to do you harm."

"What do you know about that subject?" asks Rufus.

"I've heard it on good authority," I say, a little embarrassed, "anyway, we should see if Gemma can show us the recording from yesterday on the television."

I turn and ask the crows and finches whether now is a convenient time. It is and they fly over to our house ahead of us. Rufus guides me and Oliver across the road where the cars actually stop for us. One passenger in a bright-red car points as we move across in front of them. I head up the wire trellis as Oliver and Rufus join the birds around the lounge window. Gemma has seen us coming from that window and set up the machine to play the recording. Earlier, she and I moved the television as it is on a stand with wheels and now the television is facing the window.

I stand on the windowsill and ask whether everyone can see. The finches are in the front with their beaks against the glass. The ten crows can't all fit on the sill with them, let alone Rufus and Oliver.

"We'll have to have two showings, Gemma," I say, "so that they can all see."

"Good idea, Frederick. Perhaps we should provide popcorn for everyone," says Gemma, with a slight narrowing of her eyes.

"Yes, I'll go outside and ask them to organise so we can have two showings, and I'll wave when you can start."

I scoot outside and inform the little crowd of my fellow animals that we'll have two showings. Oliver and Rufus stand with the finches and two crows, Seb and Rob, also stand on the sill. The other crows preen themselves on the white wooden handrail around the front door or simply sunbathe, all the while listening to the reactions of Seb and Rob.

I wave at Gemma, who smiles and presses the play button. The television is about three feet from the window and so the animals have a good view of their protest.

"Is that what I look like?"

"Doesn't Jacqueline look slightly purple?"

"My tail's wonky."

"My feathers are at a different angle on the left-hand side than on the right-hand side."

"My eyes are different colours."

These are some comments I hear. There is a clamour to

replay certain parts of the program and Gemma replays these sections with a patience I am pleased to see.

The second showing is mainly for the crows, but Rufus is watching again and practising the pose he thinks he should adopt on Saturday. It is only slightly different to the one on the television, but with the important addition of a nut.

"Thank you," says Seb, "I've never seen myself on television and that's something to tell the grandkids." The other crows caw their appreciation.

"Thank you too," says Benedict, a chaffinch, "can we come and see the coverage of Saturday's event?"

"Of course," I reply, "I'm sure there will be lots of replays to see."

"Thank you," says Benedict. "I believe our extended family is intending to come and perch in the tree."

"Really? How many of them will there be?"

"Well..." says Benedict, "probably about thirty? Thirty-five?"

"The tree won't be big enough," says Rob, "the council will have to add some branches for us to use."

"We can perch on the twigs," says Ethel the finch. "I think we can all fit."

"The woodpeckers are turning up too," says Stan, "but they can attach themselves to the trunk. The starlings will come, but will take over the tree next to the one we'll be in. Verity, the head starling, thinks about two hundred will come, so this is a massive protest. I think in the eyes of the law, the starlings will be indulging in secondary picketing, but I'm not sure who has the courage to arrest two hundred starlings."

"Not me for sure," says Oliver. "Anyway, I should head back. I will see you tomorrow. Shall we say 9:30am?"

"Yes, thank you, Iver. We'll see you then," I say.

"I'll help him across the road," says Rufus. "See you all tomorrow." With that, he hops off, closely followed by Oliver, who gets across the road safely.

"We'll go too," says Ethel the finch, "we have to get organised for tomorrow."

The finches fly off, leaving the crows and myself.

"Freddie," says Reg, "look who's over there on the fence."

I turn to my right and see Aubrey and Arabella perched there on the top of the fence, looking very pristine.

I look in the window and beckon to Gemma to come outside as it is debriefing time. Aubrey and Arabella flutter down to the front door.

"Hello, Freddie, old sport," says Aubrey in his best Jay Gatsby phrasing, "how are things going?"

"They're going well," I replied. "We're preparing for our tree protest tomorrow."

"There's a lot of interest in that," says Arabella, "be careful about associating Mary and John with this house on TV footage or in a photo."

"Right," says Gemma, "that's a good idea. I hope everything is going to be okay for them."

"It should be fine," says Aubrey, "so much so that they're going to be invited to Amsterdam in three weeks' time to attend a special event at the Van Gogh Museum. This is a lot earlier than we thought we'd invite them. You will also be invited as there's something we'll need you to help us with at

Europoort. I can't say any more for now, but you could well be working with Cornelius, Bertie, and Johann. Cornelius has a nose for finding things and he's unearthed a racket we need to put a stop to."

"That's wonderful," says Gemma, looking at me. "What do you think, Frederick?"

"I think it will be fine. I'm glad Cornelius will be involved, and I'm intrigued by what Bertie and Johann will be doing. Untying knots and accuracy in throwing nuts will be important parts of what we're doing."

Aubrey smiles but says nothing.

He and Arabella then gave us a long update on what the results of our surveillance had been in Amsterdam. Apparently, the cyclists of Alkmaar were overwhelmed with their charitable donations. The bee population had increased in Utrecht, which now had many bus shelters with bee-friendly plants on their roofs. The people we'd followed were all being processed in the judicial system and had found that they could no longer afford the most expensive lawyers as the funds in their bank accounts had been reduced by an unknown protagonist who left no trace of their identity.

Gemma tries not to look pleased with herself and fails.

"Do you know whether any of the organisations associated with the people we followed know about where we live?" I ask.

"There's no evidence of that, Freddie," says Arabella, "none."

"There was someone observing the house from a car when we were away," says Gemma. "Do you know who that was?"

"Yes, he was working with Europol and monitoring the house whenever Mrs Elkins was away. He says there was nothing suspicious at all going on, but that the crows around here are observant and recognised him wherever he parked, even in the library car park. You have some outstanding friends, Gemma and Freddie," replies Arabella.

"That's good," says Gemma. "I'm reassured by that, thank you. What happened to that dratted kingfisher, by the way?"

"He's on one of the Friesian islands in solitary confinement."

"And he couldn't have contacted anyone and told them our address?" persists Gemma.

"Frank, at no time knew your address, so there are no worries in that regard."

Gemma looks relieved and glances at me.

"If we go back to Amsterdam, will there be assassins after me?" I ask, "because I'm wondering whether I'll have to be dyed again as that might confuse John and Mary. We might have to tell them what we did when they were away in the Maldives. They'd surely realise I'd changed colour and would want to know why."

Aubrey smiles: "We have no plans to dye either you, Freddie, or Gemma, so there's no need to worry about. It's just one mission for perhaps half a day and that's it."

I nod with relief as I quite like my fur the way it is and I know Gemma likes her fur too, as she's always washing it.

"When will John and Mary get their invitation?" I ask.

"It will arrive on Monday," says Arabella, "the letter will state that their name was pulled out of a hat. Mrs Elkins found two cans of Heineken in the fridge when she was looking after the house. The letter will say it's from Heineken and that they've won a weekend away in Amsterdam with a special invitation to attend a gala event at the Van Gogh Museum and then a larger celebration in the evening at The Rijksmuseum."

"Yes, Mary likes to drink lager sometimes, whereas John likes spirits," I say.

"Interesting," says Arabella, "we'll have to remember that detail."

"Will we go on the train again?" asks Gemma. "I liked that journey. It was quite peaceful and straightforward. What about you, Freddie?"

"There was certainly plenty of time to read," I say. "I hope we can travel like that again."

"From here, it's probably just as quick to go on the train as it is to fly on a plane," says Aubrey, "so we'll book you on the train and give you each a cat carrier like last time."

"Good, that's good, anyway we should go," says Arabella, "and let you prepare for your star turn tomorrow. I expect to see you two on the television, with all your friends in the tree. Don't make any commitments until John and Mary get their letter stating the days you'll be away."

"Right," I say, "Au revoir, Arabella and Aubrey and good luck."

The two crows zoom away and are soon replaced by the local crows, who are eager to discuss the events of the following today, particularly if Gemma and I can't get out of the house in time.

We produce a few plans and decide we'll try to be in the

park at 9:30am, as agreed with Oliver. We'll have to miaow and scratch at the front door if John and Mary aren't awake in time and the kitchen window is closed for any reason.

Gemma and I wish the crows a good evening and head inside. Gemma is now an expert climber and can pull herself up the trellis better than I can, although I pass the time of day with the Lancashire Rose, cacti, and primroses who appreciate social niceties more than Gemma realises.

We both have a snack before Gemma trots off to read her book on Stoicism. I head back upstairs and carefully pull out a book on *The Bible* by Karen Armstrong from the top row of the bookshelf. I have to stand on my back paws on the back of the couch and reach upwards to hook the book with a claw and ease it out of its snug place between *Trainspotting* by Irvine Welsh and *Frankenstein* by Mary Shelley.

Ms Armstrong is really rather good at telling a story, even a long-winded one such as the biography of The Bible and I find the story quite compelling, although there are so many names with which I am unfamiliar. I fall asleep and dream I live in an ancient monastery somewhere in deepest, darkest Egypt where I am a monk translating the Bible from Greek into Latin by the light of candles. Unfortunately, the hot wax from my candle sets fire to my parchment and most of my translation is lost to posterity, in fact the only words left of mine in the whole of the book are 'Dominus Flevit' or in English 'Jesus Wept'. A small but important contribution.

Chapter 6

Today

I WAKE UP FEELING EXCITED as today is the today when we can start to make a difference, as long as we can get out of the house, of course. I check the kitchen window and it's open so we can at least use our normal route to the park. I'm hoping Mary and John will come with us, so it might be better if we use the front door, as I fear our human parents may be too heavy for the trellis. The front door is locked, but I think if I hang around on the doormat looking hopeful, then perhaps at least Mary might get the message. John is not really a morning person but will probably follow Mary if she comes with us.

Gemma scoots into the lounge.

"Freddie, Freddie, Mary is already awake and getting dressed in her outdoor clothes, so I think she might be coming with us." Gemma looks quite excited, and I hope she's alright as I have never seen her so enthusiastic.

There is a crash from John's room, which indicates he, too, is at least trying to get dressed. I think he might have put both his lower limbs down one trouser leg and fallen onto the bed as a result. He wasn't a flamingo in a previous life, as he doesn't have a sense of balance, although to be fair, flamingos don't wear trousers, at least not in the nature documentaries I've seen. This information about our human parents is encouraging, and we dash downstairs for some breakfast. Mary has already put the kibbles out and is ladling out some wet food into our bowls.

"You two kitties will need your strength today if you're climbing a tree and the slide, so I've given you some extra wet food. Now the tree inspection is at ten o'clock, so we should leave here around 9:30am and this should give you plenty of time to meet your friends. We don't want the council to cut the tree down, do we? I've even written a sign."

I'm so happy that I rub myself around Mary's legs for two whole minutes to show my gratitude. Gemma looks happy and allows Mary to stroke her head for almost ten seconds, which is a record in my experience. Mary shows us her sign which says "Leave the tree alone" with some nice renditions of leaves in purple crayon. It looks vaguely autumnal.

I compose myself and try not to eat too quickly. The clock says 8:30, so we have an hour before we leave, plenty of time to treat my kibbles with individual respect.

Heavy footsteps on the ceiling indicate John is now walking around and not falling over, so perhaps they'll both come with us after all. I look at Gemma and she is chewing her wet food with great gusto and seems to be enjoying it.

"Do you think I should have another go on the slide?" she asks after completing her meal.

"I think so, even if you stop at the bottom and then leap off in that athletic manner of yours," I say encouragingly.

Gemma actually landed further away than I did using this method, even though I had momentum from the slide.

"What about the swings? Have you been on them? Would I be able to balance on one?"

"Yes, the key thing with the swing is to climb onto it slowly when it's still and not to leap onto it as then your momentum makes the swing move and you're more likely to fall off."

"Which isn't good is it?" says Gemma thoughtfully, "yes, that's good advice. Anyway, I might do that after we've saved the tree."

"In celebration?"

"Yes, definitely in celebration."

After I finish my breakfast, I run upstairs to peer out of the window towards the park and I can see a number of cars on the road where normally there are none at the weekend. I realise that the event today might be more popular than I'd realised, and I hope people will let us through so we can sit in the tree.

I decide to try to relax for a few minutes, so I start to read a book about the Zulu War and two decisive battles on 22nd January 1879 called Isandlwana and Rorke's Drift, which had very different outcomes for the Zulu Nation. I'm glad I wasn't travelling with the British Army at that time, as I might not have survived. A lieutenant called John Chard was at Isandlwana on the morning of 22nd January but headed over to Rorke's Drift where he was one of the leaders of the defence of this outpost and received the highest medal for bravery that British soldiers could win. If he'd stayed at

Isandlwana, he would have probably died. Such is the fickle nature of life. I'm not hoping to win a medal for my defence of the nice tree in the park. I'm doing it because I reckon trees are a good thing for the planet and can do many things other than become toilet paper for humans to use.

Gemma trots into the room and looks at my choice of reading material.

"It's not like you to read war books. Are you expecting trouble today?"

"No, I decided to read this book, as it seems to be new on the shelves."

"Yes, well, you should put it down, as Mary and John are going to come with us. They're going to carry us across the road too, which will be very kind of them."

"Will you let them carry you?"

"Yes," sniffs Gemma, "as long as it's Mary and not John. He sometimes drops his coffee cup on the pavement in the morning on his way to work. He's not dropping me on the pavement or on the road, for that matter."

Mary and John appear in the room at this point and watch us as we wait eagerly by the front door. Mary is wearing her red pullover and jeans. John is wearing his favourite denim jacket and blue corduroys. They put on their outdoor shoes and open the door. Gemma scoots out straight away and I follow her at a more leisurely stroll. John takes out his keys to lock the door behind us but drops them on the steps.

"See what I mean?" whispers Gemma. "That could have been me."

John locks the door, and we head out through our garden

gate and up a slight bank to the side of the road. Gemma walks close to Mary and, sure enough, Mary picks her up and looks both ways. John glances at me and I miaow indicating he can give me a lift if he wants. John picks me up gently and we all cross the road together.

As we crest the slight rise to the park, we all see that the park is rather full. Gemma looks at me and nods at the tree. Oliver is already sitting on a branch along with the crows and finches. Wilf is pointing at the tree and people are taking pictures of all the animals. The camera crews are fine tuning their equipment. Some adults have brought a barbecue with them and are setting it up on the grass, which seems dangerous as there hasn't been too much rain recently. People have positioned themselves around the slide and are awaiting the star of that particular show who hasn't shown up yet. I look over John's shoulder and see Rufus heading down his tree, carrying an acorn with him. He practises holding the acorn in a heroic pose before crossing the road. Gemma agitates to be let down to the ground and I miaow at John so he can place me on the ground too.

"Hello, Rufus," I say, "your fans are waiting for you by the slide."

"Morning, Freddie and Gemma," he replies. "I know. There's a lot of them. I'll scamper down there, do a few jumps, and then scoot back up to the tree. Hopefully, people will follow me from the slide."

"The wasps are doing a good job of displaying the focal point of this morning's event," says Gemma. "You can't miss them."

"Yes, they're auditioning for a job with the council to work in road works directing traffic," I say. "They'd be good at that."

"We should join Oliver," says Gemma, looking at Mary in the hope she will follow us.

Rufus goes over to the slide and Gemma and I scamper to the tree, followed by Mary and John, who are talking to each other about how busy the park is and that it is down to their two cats. They're proud of us. Gemma sits on her back legs and leaps into the tree, receiving a round of applause from the twenty humans who are there. The TV cameras start heading our way. I don't possess as much spring in my back legs as Gemma, so I climb up the trunk of the tree using the technique I learned from Rufus. I swerve to avoid two nuthatches and three woodpeckers who are perched on the tree already.

"Freddie, you're here," squawk the crows in unison and they make a lot of noise. The starlings in the next tree take off and carefully avoiding Wilf, perform two complete murmurations, a whirl of close-formation flying where they create three-dimensional shapes in the sky before they land back in the tree again. Not to be outdone, the five Wilf arrows zoom around the park three times before pointing at the tree again.

"Things are livening up," says Oliver, "now that you've arrived, Freddie and Gemma, where are your owners?"

"Our human parents are over there looking at us and shaking their heads," replies Gemma. "They feel responsible for all these people and animals being here."

I smile at how perceptive Gemma is.

The TV camera crews come closer as the van from the council circles around the park looking for a space. We all crane our necks to discover where the van is going. Eventually, the driver lets out his two passengers, who walk over towards the tree.

"They won't be too happy having to walk an extra fifty yards," suggests Gemma, glaring at the two women who are wearing high visibility jackets and black trousers. "I reckon they don't exercise as much as they could do."

"Not everyone can exercise as much as they would like to," I reply.

Rufus arrives and climbs up the trunk, saying hello to the woodpeckers and nuthatches before joining us on the branch. The humans show their placards, including Mary, whose crayon drawing looks better from further away, like some Impressionist paintings I've seen in an enormous book in the library. As is the way of the universe, I see Angela from the library walking in the crowd. She now has orange hair. I wave at her when she looks towards the tree and heads over towards us.

"Freddie is that you?" asks Angela. "It is, isn't it?"

I miaow twice, showing it is definitely me twice over.

"You were on the news, weren't you? I said that to Roger the next day, and he said I was hallucinating."

I point at the written communication on the tree trunk. Angela reads it and looks disgusted.

"That's terrible. They should leave the tree alone."

I miaow and catch the TV Cameraman filming our

interaction. Now Angela will be on the news too, both here and in the Benelux countries. Roger will still accuse her of hallucinating.

"So, you're an environmentalist now, Freddie, that's good," Angela continues, "I wondered why you hadn't come to the library as much. You're out looking after this tree."

The two council representatives arrive at the tree. The children present produce their signs, and the crows squawk loudly. Wilf points at the two representatives for ten seconds before flying away to another tree to await developments. The starlings stop squabbling amongst themselves and stare at the two people.

"Are these your animals, madam?" asks one representative whose name badge says '76116 – Rita'. She is talking to Angela.

"Well, they're mostly wild animals who live in the park and use the tree for pleasure, but I know this cat here, the handsome black, grey, and white one, he's called Freddie, and he used to visit me at the library."

Gemma looks at me with a smirk before re-affixing her finest dog-hating Sneer Level seven at the officials.

"Does he have a library card?" asks the other official '72919 – Sandra'.

"He does actually," says John stepping forward, "the library gave both Freddie and Gemma cards so they can take out some books as they like looking at the pictures."

An 'ah' goes around the crowd.

"Kitty CAN read, I knew it," says a little girl.

"I wouldn't say that," says John smiling, then he glances at me and continues, "on the other hand, it wouldn't be a complete surprise if they could read."

Gemma looks at me and smiles.

"Right," says 72919 – Sandra, "well the reason we were going to remove this tree was because of the wasps and their nests, but there appears to be no room for the wasps any longer as it's full of birds and other animals, including the celebrity sliding somersaulting squirrel, so I'll remove this notice, and tell you all that the tree is no longer under threat."

There is a cheer from the humans, however, the squawking from the crows and finches goes on for longer. When this dies down, 76116 – Rita continues: "I'm pleased to say that we'll be planting six more trees in the park next week and we hope you'll all enjoy those in the weeks and months ahead."

With that, the two officials head back to the edge of the park.

"Congratulations everyone," I say, "thank you to all the crows, all the finches, the woodpeckers, the nuthatches, the cats, the squirrel, the starlings, and the wasps, everyone helped."

"Yes, we've all done this together," says Gemma and she stands up on her hind legs and taps her paws together, as though applauding everyone.

A lot of squawking and chirping and singing ensues for a minute or two.

"Well done, Freddie and Gemma," says Oliver when the noise dies down, "you're famous now."

"We're not. It's the sliding somersaulting squirrel that's

the celebrity," says Gemma, grinning at Rufus, who clutches his acorn tight to his chest.

"Yes, she was talking about me, wasn't she?" says Rufus. "Well, I'm not sure what's going to happen, but I'll try to enjoy it."

"Well done, kitties," says Mary, stroking both Gemma and me. "Your protest worked."

Gemma and I miaow in unison.

"You're the owner of these two cats?" says Samantha, "pleased to meet you. I'm Samantha and my husband Simon and I are the owners of Oliver."

"I wondered who this young cat belonged to. Pleased to meet you," replies Mary, "I'm Mary and I'm married to John, who told everyone about the cats' library cards. I wouldn't say we were the owners of these two, more like servants, especially to Gemma."

Gemma remains impassive and I presume she is counting to ten or perhaps fifty.

I scan the park and spy the adults with the barbecue.

"What are you watching?" asks Gemma.

"I'm looking at those adults with the barbecue," I reply. "They seem to have set it up in the worst possible place."

"Yes, I understand what you mean. I wonder what will happen when they switch it on?"

"We're about to find out."

The adults light the barbecue and place some food on the grille. It looks like beef burgers and steaks. As an obligate carnivore, I can't really comment on other animals eating meat, but the smell coming from the barbecue is not pleasant and I wouldn't choose to eat that kind of food. My reading shows meat eating is contributing to Climate Change as much as, if not more than, petrol-driven vehicles. The adults then move away, only occasionally glancing at the spitting food. Suddenly, a flame appears on the grass and spreads to the barbecue itself. The adults don't spot what is going on, but two children do and start hitting the flames with their protest banners and spraying water on the barbecue. Wilf sees what is happening and forms an arrow pointing at the barbecue, highlighting where the problem is occurring. Thankfully, more children see the wasps and join in, bringing the situation under control quickly. When they eventually realise what is going on, the adults appear shocked at what happened.

"Well, there's a metaphor for our times," says Gemma. "Oh, here come the interviewers for Mary and her new friend."

Sure enough, Mary and Samantha have a small forest of microphones shoved under their noses by interviewers. We face the cameras that appear above the microphones like a second line of attack. All the birds are still in the tree, and I foresee that we'll be showing them the footage being shot now for several days. I know this would please Gemma, as she enjoyed her role as a cinematographer and guide to the footage being shown.

The interviewers ask many questions, including whether Mary would consider hiring out Gemma and myself for other environmental protests in the country. Mary says she and John have never considered that. She also says that it wasn't just the three cats who'd highlighted the potential chopping down of the tree, but the crows, finches, woodpeckers, nuthatches, starlings, wasps, and above all Rufus the celebrity sliding somersaulting squirrel. Rufus holds up his acorn as if to acknowledge the mention of his name.

Then a reporter from a Dutch TV station asks a question:

"Have you seen the videos of a cat in the back of a police car in Amsterdam and performing charades at Schiphol Airport that appear remarkably similar to the female cat, Gemma?"

"I've not, no, I'm not sure how that would happen as she'd need to be held in quarantine for a long time both coming into and going out of the Netherlands and I can assure you we'd have noticed if she'd been gone for a long period."

"It looks like her," continues the reporter.

"Yes, but most calico cats appear similar because of their colouring."

Gemma looks at me with hooded eyebrows: "They're going to find out, aren't they?"

I shake my head. "I doubt it."

"When the cat's playing charades, there's another cat with her that looks like the male cat, Freddie, except he's a light-brown colour, a butterscotch or toffee colour."

Mary laughs: "Well, Freddie's not that colour and he's a normal-sized cat, so I would imagine there's a lot of other cats in Amsterdam who are the same size as Freddie who are a light-brown colour."

I miaow in agreement – I am a normal-sized cat and therefore the majority of cats are a similar size to me, even if most of them have longer front legs than I do. Luckily, I'm a clean cat and wash myself often so I can say with complete confidence that none of the light-brown colour remains on my fur.

Other interviewers have different questions, and the discussion moves away from the presence of Gemma in the Netherlands.

"There are four television companies from the Benelux countries here," says Gemma, "two from the Netherlands, one from Belgium, and one from Luxembourg. I wonder how much cross-posting of images of me there'll be now with all this publicity? Mary and John are bound to come across them."

"Yes, but no matter how many times they see them, their rational mind will say it can't be you, as you wouldn't be able to get there and back in time, as you'd be in quarantine too long."

"But the videos and images will have the date and time on them, and they'll know that they were in the Maldives on that date, so they'll always have questions."

"Well, we can't control that, can we? What will make them suspicious is us going with them to Amsterdam and us not being subjected to quarantine on that trip. We should contact Aubrey and Arabella and ask them what we should do."

"Good idea. I'll ask Stan if he can set up another meeting." She turns around and speaks to Stan, who nods in agreement.

After twenty further minutes, the reporters have exhausted their stockpile of questions, and we can move at last. Clutching his acorn, Rufus scuttles down the trunk and lollops off towards the slide. I'm not sure if he is hoping to get away from his new celebrity status or is eager to embrace it even more by putting on another show on the slide.

Some kind humans take pictures of myself and Gemma before we leave the tree and give us a stroke, thanking us for saving the tree. We miaow by way of thanks, and then trot over to where the children are being photographed with what remains of their protest placards in front of the blackened barbecue.

"Freddie, Freddie, the cat who can read," shouts a boy of about eight who is wearing a red football shirt and green shorts. He comes over and pats me on the head, as does a little girl in a brown dress. Gemma eyes the boy who says: "Can you read, kitty cat?"

Gemma miaows a loud miaow and looks at his placard, which says "Save the Tree" although the 'Save' is blackened. Gemma taps the slogan with her paw, points at the boy, and then points at the tree. The boy looks taken back and runs to his parents, but the little girl strokes Gemma and says: "Kitty says we saved the tree as much as she did." She goes to pass on the message.

"Well, at least one of them understood," says Gemma with the vague hint of a smile.

"That was effective pointing," I say. "You did well there."

"Let's have a go on the slide," says Gemma. "I could do with a bit of light relief."

We trot down the slight incline to the playground where Rufus is going through his full repertoire of jumps and somersaults, all the time being photographed by people using their phones.

We follow Rufus up the steps of the ladder and then slide down. Gemma enjoys the slide more than she lets on, as her leap from the end shows off her natural grace and athleticism. I don't stop like she does. I jump as soon as I get near to the end, hoping my momentum will take me soaring over the grass, but it never does, not even when I put my tail straight up in the air.

Mary and John come over to watch us and Mary takes out her phone and starts to video. Gemma doesn't seem to mind, but I feel self-conscious and decide to stop. John picks me up and tells me that one interviewer has said Gemma and I will be popular and that we can expect to receive many invitations to attend environmental protests as we are photogenic. This seems a superficial reason to me and ignores the reasons the protest is taking place.

Gemma has four leaps from the slide and seems to land in the same place every time. She's consistent but gets frustrated that although she is putting more effort in, she isn't jumping any further.

Rufus, Gemma, John, Mary, and I cross the road together. Rufus waves au revoir and scoots up his tree. Gemma and I wait until the front door is open to enter the house. John and Mary stay outside for a few minutes and later we saw why.

Gemma goes downstairs to do some stretching, and I retire beneath the sofa, where I read a book called *The History of the Kings of Britain* by Geoffrey of Monmouth. Geoffrey wrote this book many centuries ago. It covers the period from 1100 BC to 689 AD and includes a chapter on King Arthur, even though I've read in another book that he never existed.

We can never know for sure who is right about these historical matters, but I read the King Arthur section with a great deal of interest, although he seemed to spend most of his time killing many people in battle with his sword, Caliburn. I won't be using him as a role model, not even in my dreams. He's an anti-Buddhist figure. I fall asleep and have a strange dream where I'm fighting an unknown assailant in a tree with a sword in my left paw and all the time the crown I'm wearing keeps blocking my view. I'm woken by Gemma tapping me on the forehead.

"The evening news is on the TV, let's watch," she says, "I've set the machine to record, I'm not sure if the humans will be aware, but we should at least try, so we can show the birds and the squirrel."

"That's considerate of you," I reply. "Let's discover how we appear this time."

"I'm sure our human parents were interviewed afterwards, so it'll be interesting to find out what they said."

We position ourselves so we can see the television with an uninterrupted view. The news has started and none of it is very hopeful. There's been a forest fire, a car accident, and a bridge has been closed down because the concrete is crumbling. Then, as a bit of light relief, after the adverts, is the pet protest in the park. That's us.

John and Mary are both sitting in their own chairs and eating food from their trays. However, when the pet protest comes on the TV, they encourage Gemma and me to come closer to the screen.

"Why are you recording this, John?" asks Mary.

"I didn't know I was," replies John, looking suspiciously at Gemma, who licks her right front paw to disguise her desire to glare back at him, like she would have done only a few months ago.

Mary looks at Gemma, too.

"You don't think Gemma is recording this, surely?"

"Well, I've seen her pressing a few buttons, and she seems to follow some kind of plan, so who knows?"

Gemma's front paw is receiving a very thorough wash, though I suspect she is enjoying the verbal attention. Her pricked ears are taking it all in. Then suddenly we are on the TV. I am shocked to see myself. I look small and the tree looks large. Gemma is glaring at the camera all the time. Our interviews went well, and Mary smiles at us and even pats Gemma on the head. Gemma stares at the TV. Then there is footage of us walking back to our house. The next scene is Mary and John giving a TV interview. They say that if people would like Freddie and Gemma to help with their environmental protest, then the people should provide some information about who or what the protest is against so that Freddie and Gemma can send a message. It's entirely possible that the cats won't be able to attend in person. Gemma looks at me and seems pleased with what she heard. I would imagine she'll enjoy reading the letters. Once the news is over, Mary and John watch another program, but I can tell that Gemma wants to talk, so we scoot downstairs and pretend to have a late snack.

"Do you want to talk about the interview we just heard?" I ask her.

"Yes, I think we'll get to see the letters first because the post comes after they've both left for work. We'll find out who's writing to us, won't we?"

"There probably won't be many," I say. "I imagine you'll be able to open them with your claws in a few minutes and read them all."

"We shall see, we shall see. That's exciting and don't forget the humans will receive their Netherlands invitation on Monday too, so we'll have the exact date for that. What I'm really excited about is an idea I've had for my book."

"Oh, your book, what's the idea, the pet shop animals solve crimes?"

"Yes, they do. It's mainly the female cats who solve the problem, of course…"

"Of course, Gemma," I reply.

"But these cats can't write or type, so the rabbit writes the email dictated by the budgie."

"The rabbit does? That's inventive. What other pets will solve the crimes? The dogs?"

"Not the dogs, of course not the dogs, don't be silly. The cats, hamsters, budgies, rabbits, parrots, and guinea pigs. Plus, an occasional guest appearance from a rarer type of pet, such as a goat."

"How would the goat get out of the pet shop without the owner noticing? It wouldn't be able to get through the cat flap."

"Mm, a miniature goat? Well, during the day, the door would be open."

"I think the local wildlife could help too, such as the crows, and the jackdaws, and ravens, and the squirrels."

"Well, hold on, Freddie, it's supposed to be the pets who solve the crimes, not the local birds."

"The pets are wise enough to ask the local wildlife. I'm sure the female cats know how important local knowledge is."

"Yes, of course, they will know to do that."

"What's the title going to be?" I ask, hoping she will have thought of something suitable.

"I don't have a proper title yet, but something like the Pet Shop Detectives."

"Yes, Pet Shop Sleuths, something like that, anyway it sounds promising. I wish you the best of luck. I can be a beta reader if you wish."

"Oh, what a good idea. Thank you. I feel inspired now to start straightaway."

With that, Gemma scampers off to start her magnum opus. I think there was a TV detective once upon a time called *Magnum*, who had a big moustache. If he'd had an Irish cat that helped with his investigations, then the title for that book could have been Magnum Opus, but this spurious thought wouldn't help Gemma.

I have a quick snack and then head upstairs to continue to read Geoffrey of Monmouth's book. I know that William Shakespeare wrote about King Lear, but Geoffrey mentions him too and the fact he had three daughters: Regan, Goneril, and Cordelia. According to Geoffrey, King Lear founded Leicester on the River Soar and Cordelia buried her father under the river a few miles south of the city. This is a good story but not true, as Geoffrey says Cordelia buried Lear in a vault previously used in honour of the god Janus. But Janus is a Roman god and, according to Geoffrey, Lear died seven years before the founding of Rome in 753 BC, so this doesn't follow at all. I think about mentioning this to Gemma, so she can mention it in her book to show that pets solve all kinds of mysteries, not just murders. I decide not to read any more of Geoffrey's book and choose another called *Payment Deferred* by CS Forester. This story is about a bank employee called Marble who is a nasty character and murders a distant relative at the end of the first chapter. At least this book indicates it's fiction. CS Forester is best known for writing about a naval character called Horatio Hornblower, but the action in *Payment Deferred* is all on dry land so far. I fall asleep and dream about pets inspecting an underground cavern containing a dead king and a statue of a murderous bank clerk.

Chapter 7

Today

TODAY IS A SUNDAY, AND it's time to practise our Extra Sensory Perception on John and Mary. We're trying to get Mary to buy Hoisin Sauce and John to buy garlic, neither of which they normally buy.

Gemma and I sit on the bare chair in the kitchen and stare at the humans as they go about their 'leaving for the shops' routine. While they're out, we can show the recording of the TV news from yesterday through the front-room window to the birds and squirrel and cat, if they all remember to turn up on time. We told them 11am would be best.

As soon as Mary and John leave the house, we scoot into the lounge and manage to turn the TV towards the window. Gemma presses a few buttons, and the recording appears on the screen. She then presses fast forward to the part of the broadcast relating to the park protest and then presses pause with her paw.

I have worked out how to open the window, so when Oliver arrives with Rufus, they're able to sit on the windowsill on the inside. The sparrows and smaller birds crowd in too and the crows sit on the windowsill on the outside. Everyone is very well behaved. Gemma announces that she'll play the piece through twice, the first time at normal speed and the second time she'll take requests to stop the action as and when it's requested. Gemma presses the play button, and the story begins. The smaller birds are transfixed by the large screen and ask their neighbour whether that's what they really look like, as it's a bit of a shock to them, as they've not seen themselves before. I hadn't realised that Rufus had been holding a nut the whole time he was in the tree. I'm drawn towards Gemma's look of contempt. Once the recording is completed, Gemma returns to the start of the report and patiently goes through it, almost a frame at a time. After about a minute, Jacqueline says something:

"Freddie and Gemma, when you were away, there was a man hanging around in a car and I've just seen him in the crowd. He was there yesterday."

"I'll reverse the film and let me know when you recognise him and I'll stop," says Gemma, tapping at the remote control.

"There," says Jacqueline, "he's the one in the blue jacket just behind Cyril the finch who's sitting on that branch," and points with her wing.

It is time for me to assist, and I trot over to the screen and point at someone with my left paw.

"The one to that person's left, Freddie," says the female crow. I move my paw, and Jacqueline gives a low squawk. Gemma comes over to stand by me and stares at the screen.

"He's got brown hair, and he's white. Apart from that, he's not got many distinguishing features," says Gemma.

"He's got a largish nose and fairly small ears," says Stan.

"He should be easy to spot, as he has a small mole near his right eye," says Rufus, "and now you mention it, I reckon he was watching us on the slide."

"Let's play the report again," says Reg, "and discover whether we can recognise him somewhere else."

"Good idea, Reg," says Gemma, "don't be scared to shout out if you find him or think you see him." She presses the continue button.

After about thirty minutes, we find five further frames in which the person appears. He is wearing blue jeans and a denim jacket and appears to wear training shoes. Gemma and I can now describe him to Aubrey and Arabella. I hope this is the man they say is on our side. If he was the one who was watching the house when we were away, I'm not sure why he would be hanging around now when we had all returned home. When John and Mary are being interviewed, the camera focuses on the interviewer twice and in the second shot, the man is walking along the footpath in front of our house.

Talking of John and Mary, they will soon be back, so we should say 'au revoir' to our animal friends. We try to move the TV back to its original place but can't quite manage it exactly. I can't close the window tightly either, so Gemma and I hang around on the windowsill, pretending to be getting some fresh air.

When John and Mary return, we both take a keen interest in their purchases as we sit on the wooden chair in the kitchen. Unfortunately, John opens the fridge door and places their recycled plastic box containing their purchases behind the door so we can't discover what they've bought. He soon loads the fridge and closes the door. At the same time, Mary has placed all their bottle purchases in the overhead cupboards, so we can't see those either.

John goes downstairs to put the cardboard box away and Mary wanders into the lounge. She soon comes back looking slightly perturbed.

"What have you two kitties been up to when we were out?"

Gemma looks impassively at Mary, and I stare at the wall for about ten seconds as I am blushing under my fur. What has she spotted?

"The TV has been moved, and the window has been opened. How did you do that? The TV remote control has been moved too."

"You'll be in for a shock if they answer," says John, who's come back upstairs.

"They've been showing their animal friends last night's news broadcast. There are one or two paw prints on the windowsill."

Gemma jumps down from the chair and heads into the lounge. I decide to follow to show solidarity.

"I forgot to put the remote control back," says Gemma. "How careless of me." She shakes her head.

"The TV was pointing more towards their two chairs rather than into the middle of the room, like it is now," I reply, "and the window was closed when they left and now it's open."

"This sounds like something I should be writing for my novel," says Gemma, "like analysing a crime scene. Deductions that the pet detectives would make – could I call them petectives?"

"No, the reader will think the book hasn't been edited properly."

"Yes, you're right. Where should the TV stand have been?"

"There are some indentations in the carpet, Gemma, little depressions the wheels of the TV stand cause, because of the weight. We were about a foot away from those indentations."

"Oh yes, I see them now. I wasn't aware we'd moved the screen."

"It might have moved when we pushed the TV stand."

"I'm going to write this down, Freddie. I need to work out how to turn this scene into a murder scene and where the body would lie."

Gemma walks around the chairs and even jumps on to the windowsill. She surveys the garden and then the interior of the room.

"I have an idea. I'm going to write it down now before I forget it."

With that, she scampers downstairs, and I retire to read my *Payment Deferred* book under the couch. I finish the book at about 3pm. William Marble is a bank clerk. He is short of money. A chance visit from a well-off distant relative provides him with an opportunity to solve his financial woes. The relative is buried in the garden, but Mr Marble's guilt leads him to start drinking and gazing into the garden to make sure no one discovers his secret.

Some insider information on the imminent rise of a foreign currency allows Mr Marble to become a wealthy man. He can send his children to the best schools, buy fancy furniture, and his wife can buy the finest clothes. But the nagging fear of discovery eats away at Mr Marble and infects his relationship with this family. He starts an affair with a married woman who ends up extorting him. His son discovers the affair and is so upset he rides his motorbike into a wall. Then his wife discovers his secret, and their daughter becomes so ashamed of her parents, she leaves home.

The central character had no redeeming qualities. However, I do give credit to the writer for making him so objectionable.

If I hadn't read this book, I would associate CS Forester only with Horatio Hornblower and *The African Queen*. Now, I can understand why some critics regard Forester as the unsung godfather of English noir. I fall asleep with this thought in my head and dream a strange dream about being a ship's cat on a Royal Navy vessel at the time of the Napoleonic Wars. I smoke a pipe and possess a small cannon which fires Hoisin Sauce and garlic at our opponents.

Chapter 8

Today

AFTER EATING A HEARTY BREAKFAST, Gemma goes to write her murder / mystery novel. We agree we should wait for the post to arrive at noon as we'd both like to know whether the invitation from the Netherlands arrives for John and Mary.

I head out to meet my squirrel friend Rufus and we cross the road safely. We stand on the grassy bank on the opposite side of the road and scan around to see if the house-watching man is in a car.

"I can't find him anywhere," says Rufus, "and I wonder if that's a good thing or not. He might have felt safer in a crowd on Saturday, he could blend in, whereas today, a Monday, there's hardly anyone around, so he might be hiding."

"You'd make a good character in Gemma's murder / mystery book. You say all the right things to sow doubt in the mind of the reader."

"Gemma's writing a book. How's she doing that?"

"She's good at typing and has found out how to use John's computer when he's at work. She saw him type in his password and so she can use it whenever she wants."

"What's a password, Freddie?"

"It's a personal code known only to yourself that all secure computer applications ask you before you're allowed to use their system."

"It sounds complicated, and I'm glad I'm not online."

"Yes, there's no electricity supply in your tree – computers run on electricity."

"And they use batteries to store the electricity in case the electric power is lost for any reason. So, I could use a computer as long as someone charged the battery for me. Actually, it would be useful to keep a record of my nut consumption and the length of my leaps, although I should tell you something about that."

I take a peek around the park, as the crows should be here by now, but it seems they are dive-bombing a dog at the other end of the park and so are preoccupied.

"What's your news about jumping off the slide?"

"I'm going to stop doing it for a while and try one of the swings. The council has introduced a lighter swing. It's the one with a yellow seat and red frame on its own," he points towards the playground, "and I'm going to try swinging and discover how high I can get. It's a different technique. I was practising leaping onto the swing yesterday and I must hit it at the right angle, otherwise I'll gain no forward momentum, but I must be careful not to fall off."

"It's a good time to practise as the children are at school and so won't be trying to use the swings at the same time as you."

"Yes, that's why I'm here. Do you want to try the swings?"

"Let's go, Rufus. I want to watch you before I try."

We scamper over to the playground, and I admire the new shiny swing. Rufus stops about twelve feet away from it. I observe him closely. He stands on his hind legs and then runs at the swing, leaping so that his front paws land on it so that it moves forwards and then when it moves back, he places his back paws on it and then adjusts his body backwards and forwards at the appropriate times. He is able to move for about twenty seconds. He then encourages me to try. I copy his technique and run at the swing. I leap but fly over the top of it.

I stare at the slide for about ten seconds as I am embarrassed. I trot back to my starting point and charge at the swing. This time I hit it quite hard so that it moves further forward than I was expecting, so I overbalance and fall off. I try again and didn't hit the swing quite as hard, so I can perch on it, but don't move far before I stop completely.

Rufus tries again and swings for twenty seconds, more or less the same as last time. He looks pleased and takes a longer runup the next time. He hits the swing hard with plenty of momentum and flies quite high but remains calm and holds on to one of the chains and manages to gain some momentum coming backwards too, but then the smoothness of the plastic causes him to miss his footing, and he falls off. Rufus displays a cat-like ability to land on his paws.

We both try three more times at swinging further but are unable to improve on our initial attempts. By the time we finish, the crows visit us.

"Freddie and Rufus how are you?" asks Seb.

"I'm exhausted," says Rufus, "getting a swing to swing is a difficult thing."

"Rufus is right," I say. "It's more physically demanding than sliding down a slide. What was going on with that dog?"

"It was a careless dog-walker letting his canine off its lead," says Jacqueline, "the dog was running around chasing everything including us when we were trying to catch a few worms, so as you can imagine we weren't too pleased about that."

"Yes, that dog received a proper pecking," says Stan, "and we bombed the owner too, as they're the ones who are really at fault and not the dog."

"Did they put the dog on the lead?" I ask.

"They did eventually. They took the hint," replies Rob. "It takes some people a few minutes to get the picture."

"Like a slowly developing print taken on an old camera," says Rob.

"That's philosophical," says Rufus, "and poetic too."

"Thank you," replies Rob. "You used rhymes earlier in this conversation."

"Yes, I'm thinking of getting a computer now that Gemma's started writing her own novel. I'll write down a few poems and keep a record of my nut consumption."

The crows look at each other and then at me. I frown under my fur.

"Rufus, where are you going to get a computer from?" I ask. "You do realise that computers cost quite a bit of money?"

"I knew there'd be a problem. Do your human parents possess one I could borrow?"

"Well, I suppose you could borrow Mary's small laptop that she takes on holiday, which she doesn't use at other times of the year. You could come to the house and use it during the day. Gemma can carry it in her mouth. It's quite light. We can plug it into the wall when you're using it, so the battery doesn't drain."

"Oh, that sounds great," says Rufus. "I'm not sure I can type well, but I suppose I'd get better with practice."

"Talking of coming to your house, Freddie, Arabella and Aubrey should be arriving around 1pm," says Stan.

"Thank you, Stan. It'll be interesting to discover what arrives in our mail today, so I should be going soon."

"The invitation for John and Mary will be arriving today from the Netherlands," says Rob.

"That's correct, Rob," I say, "plus there might be a few letters from people wanting us to help with environmental demonstrations."

"The last post on a Saturday is normally noon," says Jacqueline, "so there might not be any letters today, but there will be some tomorrow, I'm sure."

"Oh, I didn't know that," I say. "I understood there were collections every day."

"No longer," says Reg, "there used to be, but not anymore."

"Well, we'll see what happens," I reply. "I should concentrate on living in the moment and not get ahead of myself."

"Wise words, young Freddie, as usual," says Stan, "wait a

second. What's happening over there? Isn't that Oliver those men are chasing?"

"It is," I say, "let's go and help Iver before he's captured."

We all scoot to the top end of the park where Oliver is managing to evade capture, even though one of the men is carrying a net on a pole and swiping at Oliver in what seems a haphazard way. The crows split into two groups and started diving at the men, who suddenly have more to worry about than previously. I manage to reach Oliver.

"What happened, Oliver? Where did those men come from?"

"I spotted you in the park with Rufus and came out to say hello, but they were waiting for me and blocked off my path of retreat. There's one waiting by the house too, and two others were chasing me in the park."

I glance over and spot a man standing outside Oliver's residence. I shout at Reg to get the crows to bomb this man, too. Three crows peel off from attacking the man with the net and dive bomb the house watcher. Rufus has zipped up an oak tree and throws acorns at the man and although he isn't as accurate as Johann in Amsterdam, he gives the man another angle of attack to protect himself from.

"Once the man moves, you should go back inside and stay there," I say.

"I will, but you should do the same as they might be after you as well."

I haven't considered this and so keep out of sight. I've been a bit naïve in the playground and berate myself for not taking more care of me, Freddie cat.

~ 125 ~

The two men in the park are now being bothered by the starlings too and decide to retreat to their vehicle, a small white van from a hire company. A small yellow arrow suddenly appears three feet above the house watcher's head.

"That man's going to move very soon, Iver," I say. "You should get ready to head home. We'll be in touch."

"You take care, Freddie cat," says Oliver. "I'll meet you soon."

Sure enough, the wasps descend on the man's head, and he runs towards the hire van, waving his arms around like someone semaphoring an urgent message. I memorise the number plate as Oliver scoots into his garden and uses the cat flap. As the van speeds away, the wasps regroup in front of me.

"Freddie cat," choruses Wilf, "we hope you are well. We reckon you are in danger of being catnapped and would like to offer our services in escorting you home. You should return now."

"I agree with them," says Rufus, "let's go."

The crows squawk their agreement, and we move away in unison towards the road and, hopefully, towards safety.

"Have you seen those men before, Wilf?" I ask the wasps.

"Wilf believes one of them, the one with the denim jacket, was here on Saturday," choruses Wilf, "but the other two we've not seen before."

"Was the one in the denim jacket the same person who watched the house when we were away?"

"No, Freddie," says Jacqueline, swooping down to hop along beside me, "he's a different person, but Wilf's right, the man in the denim jacket was here on Saturday. There were quite a few humans wearing denim on Saturday."

As we approach the road, the wasps, whose numbers have grown, form themselves into a large square and place themselves above the road, causing a car to slow down to a halt. The square becomes an arrow pointing at the driver. We jog across the road and the arrow rearranges itself into a large thumb pointing towards the sky. Once everyone is safely across, I thank everyone for their help. The crows, starlings, and wasps say they will keep a lookout for me in the morning and report any suspicious human activity to me whilst I am still in the garden. I thank them profusely and they fly away.

I climb up the trellis and enter the kitchen, anxious to tell Gemma what has happened. She is having a snack and seems happy enough, as she is chewing her food properly rather than swallowing it whole in an impatient manner. We may be what we eat, but the way we eat is important too, and it shows how we're feeling about ourselves and what our state of mind is. She glances across at me.

"You appear to want to tell me something," she says, "shall we go upstairs and wait under the letter box? It's about time for the postwoman to make her delivery."

We sit on either side of the letter box, and I tell Gemma about Oliver's involuntary adventure with the three men in the park.

"There's a lesson for you, Frederick," she says, "there'll probably be waiting for you too, so be careful when you go out next."

I tell Gemma about the early-warning systems that are in

place and how effective Wilf has been at making a potential catnapper understand the error of his ways. Gemma says she is glad Wilf is on our side, and I have to agree with her completely.

Then a shadow looms through the small glass panes in the front door. Two envelopes drop onto the mat between us. We stare at each other, almost with disappointment. Gemma paws at the envelopes so we can find out the addressees. One envelope has a Dutch postmark and is addressed to Mary and John. We will have to witness them opening this envelope to discern their reaction. The other envelope is addressed to Gemma and Freddie and seems to be written in green crayon.

"Well, let's discover who's written to us," says Gemma, flexing her claws.

"Yes, let's read our letter," I say. "Arabella and Aub will be here at 1pm, so we have a bit of time before then."

"Should we keep these letters private?" asks Gemma, "you know, hide them from the humans, or do we leave the letters lying around so they can find them?"

"I don't see how we'll be able to hide all the letters that arrive, so we might as well leave it for them to see but make it obvious we opened the letter."

"You're expecting stacks of letters?" asks Gemma, filleting the envelope with one of her front-right claws that she sharpens daily on a scratching post bought for the purpose by Mary and John.

"I am. We might be popular."

We open the neatly folded piece of lilac paper inside.

==========

"The problem is the cursive writing," says Gemma, "I wasn't aware people still wrote letters using a biro or a fountain pen."

I study the letter quite hard and all I can read is: "Dear Freddie and Gemma: Thank you for the great example you've…" and then the rest of it I'm not sure about although it appears we've been invited to an environmental protest in somewhere that looks like Sopwith Harcourt, but Gemma can't find this place in the index of the road atlas. Either we've misread the place name or there isn't a road near the place, in which case we'll have great difficulty getting there.

"Do you think we need glasses?" asks Gemma. "Is this one of those days when you suddenly realise you're getting old?"

"You're four," I say. "You're not old. It's the writing that's causing us both a problem."

"Four years for a cat is about thirty-two in human terms," replies Gemma, "so requiring glasses is not completely unexpected."

"We should ask Aubrey and Arabella. They'll be here soon," I say. "Let's see if they can read the letter."

"Yes," says Gemma. "They're younger than us. Let's see if they can decipher this spidery writing."

"This word here," I say, pointing at the letter, "it looks like 'stethoscope', but I'm not sure about the surrounding words."

"Let me read that," says Gemma, "…I see what you mean. Could it be stepmother, or Schopenhauer or something similar?"

"We should leave it until we know what all the words are. Let's wait for the crows."

"Right," says Gemma, "I hope the other letters we get are easier to read than this one, otherwise we won't be able to get through many of them per day."

"It's a pity we can't get people to send us emails," I say.

"We're not supposed to give away secrets about our computer usage," says Gemma severely, "we're not online, pets don't have email addresses, that's what we want people to think."

There is a twin tapping at the window. We trot over and jump on to the windowsill to see Arabella and Aubrey looking very distinguished on the other side. I gesture for them to hop away and open the window slightly so they can enter the room with ease. I then close the window for practice and push my paw against the window to make sure it won't open unexpectedly.

"Hello, Arabella, hello, Aubrey," says Gemma. "Welcome to our house."

"Good to see you both," says Arabella, "you're both looking well."

"It's good to see you again, Gemma and Freddie," says Aubrey. "Did the letter arrive this morning for Mary and John?"

"It did," I reply. "It's lying on the mat. This came too..." and I grab the letter addressed to us, "...can you read it?"

Gemma frowns at me and will probably refer to me as 'Frederick' the next time she mentions me.

"Dear me, who wrote this, a drunken spider?" says Aubrey, "I can't read that, can you 'bella?"

"You've got it upside down, Aubrey," replies Arabella,

"humans start their letters with a greeting..." she turns the letter around, "...but this is... de de de... dear Freddie and Gemma, thank... thank you for the great example you are... that's about all I can read," continues Arabella. "They're inviting you to attend a protest against something."

"That's what Frederick and I understood," says Gemma curtly, "so now that's out of the way. What exciting news do you have for us?" She rubs her front paws together as if to emphasise her keenness.

"Well, Gemma and Freddie, in three short weeks you'll be heading back to the Netherlands," begins Aubrey, "Mrs Elkins will be taking you two on the train, separate from Mary and John, but you will all be staying in the same place..."

"Miep's place, she can't wait to see you..." interjects Arabella.

"...and you'll be taken to an 'environmental protest' near Europoort when Mary and John go to the Van Gogh Museum to have a look at their exhibition, which will be the greatest exhibition of his work there's ever been and then they'll head over to the Rijksmuseum where you'll join them later in the evening once the 'protest' is over."

"The protest is about a British company building a big plastic producing factory at Europoort, even though we have it on good authority that the factory is going to Antwerp," says Arabella, "however what you'll really be doing is searching a ship to find human cargo who are being trafficked into Europoort we believe. Your friend Cornelius sniffed them out last time, but only when they were on the dockside and not on the ship. We had them followed and we have the network ready to roll up on the Dutch side, but we need the ship and the shipping line too and this is where you come in…"

I glance at Gemma, who is wide-eyed with anticipation.

"…we know the ship and it's heading back to Europoort and will be docking on the day you're arriving. What we need you to do, along with Cornelius, Johann, and Bertie is find the people on the ship and release them from their bonds if at all possible, or if not raise an alarm, and we'll come and get them and arrest the crew. The shipping line has another ship running the same route and we think it's shipping human cargo, too."

"The other ship is a week behind, so we won't be able to prevent them from finding out about the capture of the vessel," says Aubrey, "and they'll be in international waters, so we can't board them and search for their human cargo."

"Any questions?" asks Arabella.

I put my paw in the air: "I do, we're worried that Mary and John might become suspicious about our previous trip to Amsterdam, if we're not put into quarantine on this next trip to Amsterdam, so how do we stop them getting suspicious?"

Arabella nods before replying.

"We're going to tell them that you have to travel separately from them, so you can receive a special 'express' quarantine check performed by an expert vet, a rapid evaluation, if you like, undertaken in a special compartment of the train. This is more or less true, of course."

Gemma looks a bit sceptical, but it seems plausible to me.

"Do you feel better, Gemma?" I ask.

"Yes. They'll probably believe what they're told. I'd like to ask why Cornelius, Bertie, and Johann are involved?"

"Cornelius is the muscle of the operation. You are the stealth element. Bertie can untie almost any knot, and Johann is a very accurate thrower of small, sharp objects. He'll distract any guards, Cornelius can bite them if necessary, you'll find where the people are held, and Bertie can untie their hands or steal the keys if that is required," replies Aubrey.

"The squirrels are very adept at evaluating situations quickly and accurately," says Arabella, "and work really well together, like you two do."

"This all sounds very promising," I say. "How many humans will there be on the ship as crew?"

"We estimate there'll be twenty crew members and perhaps thirty or so people being trafficked."

"That's a lot of people," says Gemma. "What are we supposed to do with them all?"

"Find the people on the ship, untie them if necessary, come and tell us, then lead us to them. Once we find the people on the ship, we can arrest the crew, as the people will have been held against their will on board their vessel. We have to find the people on board the vessel to prove they have been trafficked."

"That's a lot of responsibility for us," I say, "but I'm sure we can do as you want. It seems to me that the crew might try to let the people go if they feel that they're going to be arrested."

"You're thinking ahead, Freddie, that's good," says

Arabella, "that is a possibility, but I'm sure Cornelius would work out what to do. I think you might have to think on your paws too, regarding what to do."

Gemma smiles. "This sounds like fun; I'm looking forward to it greatly."

"That's good to hear, Gemma," says Aubrey, "and Freddie, you seem enthusiastic, too."

"Yes, I'm looking forward to it," I say. "It's going to be an interesting exercise for us."

Arabella and Aubrey then go over the details with us of the date and time of our departure, who would be going where and when. These details will be shared with Mary and John later in the month. The crows also tell us that the Europol man as well as his assistant are continuing to hang around until we leave for the Netherlands and that they will only depart once we return from Amsterdam. This is purely a precaution, and they were at the protest on Saturday. They were being thorough by mingling with people, just to make sure there were no known criminals present and that no one tried to harm us, even checking that our human parents were safe when being interviewed by a reporter near the house. We were relieved to hear this. When this has all been discussed, we bid farewell to Aubrey and Arabella. We both start looking forward to seeing Mrs Elkins again and Gemma is already planning to get to know all the different parts of a ship, so she'll be aware of exactly where she is at all times. She heads downstairs to find out more straightaway. I go back to my new book called *The Card* by Arnold Bennett underneath the couch, having agreed with Gemma to lurk in the vicinity of the front door at 6pm when Mary comes home, so we can observe how she reacts to the letter. I have pawed it into prominence on the front doormat with our already opened letter nonchalantly placed ever so slightly to one side.

==========

At 5:58pm, Gemma trots across The Lounge floor and installs herself in a good place on a chair where she can observe the front doormat in comfort. I spy from underneath the couch. We hear the keys turn in the lock and Mary appears, looking slightly flustered but nonetheless happy to be home. She pats Gemma on the head and says, "Hello, Freddie." I stare at the letter on the mat, which Mary has already stood on twice when taking off her blue jacket and putting it on a peg next to her purple umbrella. After taking off her shoes, she wanders into the kitchen and puts on the kettle for some restorative tea.

"That was a non-event," says Gemma. "I was hoping for some reaction at least, rather than her tap dancing on the envelope without noticing."

"John will be here soon," I reply, "although he tends not to notice either."

Sure enough, when John arrives about five minutes later, he ignores the letters completely and takes off his shoes in the lounge, before heading to his bedroom to deposit them on a shoe rack and place his bag on a chair like he normally does.

"Right," says Gemma. She scampers over to the letters and grabs them with her mouth before depositing them, one each, on John's and Mary's chairs.

"That should do it," she says.

"Let's hope so," I reply, "although it does make it obvious

we've put the letters on the chairs, as the post lady couldn't throw them that far or that accurately."

"Mm," says Gemma, "yes, it's a bit too obvious, isn't it?" She grabs the letters again and puts them back on the mat but paws the lounge door wide open so that anyone coming from the kitchen will see the post.

Mary appears clutching a mug of tea and puts it on a side table by her chair. She heads back to the kitchen. We hear some conversation and then John reprises Mary's actions. He glances at me under the couch. I miaow and look meaningfully at the front door.

"Are you cold?" he asks. "Shall I close the door?"

Gemma has heard enough and goes over to stand on the door mat.

"Oh, there's some post. Well done, Gemma," says John, trying to stroke Gemma, who sidesteps his lunge. He picks up the two envelopes instead.

John stares at his envelope for a few seconds and then looks at the back. For what, I'm not sure, perhaps a return address? He then sees our opened letter.

"Oh, I see," he says, "you two kitties have had your first fan mail, which you've opened but presumably can't read. Let's have a look…. Dear Freddie and Gemma: Thank you for the great example you've set us all, we'd like to invite you to…oh my what does this say…Mary, do you have a sec I'm trying to read the cats' fan mail to them but the writing's really messy."

Mary comes through clutching a tray and puts that next to her mug on the table. She walks over and looks at the letter. "I can't read this, I need my glasses, but I'm going to eat first… On second thoughts, Gemma's death stare tells me I should read it now… hold on Gemma…" she returns a few seconds later. "Okay, Dear Freddie and Gemma: Thank you for the great example you've set us all, we'd like to invite you to a… an environmental protest in Southampton on the 28th June against a new oil refinery being built. Then there's a return postal address and an email address and then it's signed Scotty and Frances with two paw prints, dogs by the look of it."

"Dogs?" splutters Gemma. "Writing to us? Inviting us to a protest?"

"It's their owner's writing," I say. "They can protest too."

"Yes, but they're still pretending to be dogs, yappy, barking dogs."

"What's this other envelope?" asks Mary.

"That's for us," replies John, "not for the kitties."

"It's from Holland," says Mary, "why this sudden interest from Holland?"

John takes the envelope and opens it with his finger. Gemma looks dismissive of his effort.

He takes the letter out and reads it to himself before saying, "Oh."

"Oh, what?" says Mary, taking the letter.

"We've been invited to an exhibition at the Van Gogh museum in Amsterdam and then a gala evening at the Rijksmuseum, all expenses paid, and the cats have been invited too."

"Our email was selected…" reads Mary. "What? Again? And how did they know we have cats?"

There is a knock at the door.

John goes to see who it is.

"Do come in," we hear him say.

Samantha comes into the room looking a little flustered.

"Hello, Samantha," says Mary, "are you okay?"

"I am, but I wanted to thank your wonderful Freddie cat for helping Oliver today."

Gemma tilts her head to one side and looks at me rather quizzically.

"What did Freddie do?" asks John.

"My next-door neighbour, who worked from home today, told me that Oliver went out to the park, but then he was set upon by three men who tried to catnap him, but Freddie and the crows…"

"…and the starlings and the wasps…" I say to Gemma.

"…they made the men go away, so thank you, Freddie."

I miaow and look at the wall for ten seconds as I am a bit embarrassed under my fur.

"So that's what he gets up to when we're away, is it?" asks Mary, knowing full well that is what I get up to when they're away.

"Yes, Freddie should be careful. We don't want him getting catnapped, do we?" says Samantha. "By the way, Mary, did you get the Hoisin sauce I recommended?"

I look at Gemma, who smiles an enigmatic smile and starts gazing at Mary.

"I did," says Mary. "I'm going to use it with a stir fry. John bought some garlic, and we'll probably have chicken with that."

Gemma stops gazing at Mary and looks at me with something approaching incredulity. I look at the wall again because something odd is going on and it is embarrassing. It is Arthur Koestler's fault.

Samantha comes over to me and strokes me on the head. I purr, of course, as being stroked is a good thing. Samantha says her goodbyes and then leaves.

"Well, Frederick the cat," says John, "just be careful out there." Then he goes to get some food.

Mary moves over to her chair, sits down, and reads the letter again before starting on her food.

"Who's a clever boy then?" says Gemma.

"It was the wasps that made the difference," I reply. "They were mesmerisingly efficient and organised. As were the crows who bombed the would-be catnappers."

"They're avian Stukas," says Gemma, "formidable opponents with a very steep dive."

Gemma knows more about blitzkrieg than I do, so I have to agree with her.

"I wonder what our next thought transfer experiment should be?" I say, "should it be food or something else abstract, like a yellow flowerpot? And we should wait until they're about to go shopping and receptive to purchasing ideas. Gazing at them now won't do much good."

"Right, I see. That makes sense. Let's go with a yellow flowerpot," says Gemma. "That's something we can't miss."

I retire under the couch and listen to Mary and John discussing their forthcoming trip to the Netherlands and wondering how they've been selected and whether we cats would really be able to join them as they don't want us to be placed in quarantine. Gemma listens for a while too and then heads downstairs to continue with her pet detective story.

I continue to read about *The Card*, a human, not a playing card, who is a bit of a chancer who always lands on his feet and is able to make his way in the world. I fall asleep and dream that I have been catnapped by a pack of playing cards who demand a ransom for me, which Gemma pays by winning at roulette at the casino and then at blackjack. Just as the ransom is paid, the crows swoop down and carry off the cards. Gemma keeps the money and opens a pet shop that doesn't sell dogs.

Chapter 9

Today

GEMMA AND I HAVE HAD a good day so far, she's written another chapter in her book, and I've been over the road to the park with an escort of various creatures and neither did I get catnapped, nor did we see anyone who looked as though they wanted to catnap me. Mind you, the wasps were out in numbers and are very observant. There were more of them than yesterday.

We wait for the post and sit on either side of the letter box in anticipation of a few more letters being delivered to us than the one that arrived yesterday.

At 12:03pm, the shadow of the post lady looms through the glass panels of the front door. She opens the outer flap of the letter box. A solid pile of letters lands on the doormat, bound together tightly by a red elastic band, followed by another solid pile of letters, bound together tightly by a blue elastic band. Elastic bands? We hadn't reckoned on elastic bands. We look at each other in a disappointed manner. The letters are addressed to us, or one of us at least, but the bands need snapping. Gemma gets to work with her claws and tries to saw the blue band in half, but this proves trickier than expected until she gets a single claw stuck in the band and fillets it so that the band weakens and snaps in two. There are eighteen letters in all.

I am not as adept at using my claws as Gemma, as she slits open fourteen letters during the time it takes me to open four. Once all eighteen are open, we take out the letters, place them in a neat pile, and read them. Thankfully, some people own printers connected to their computers and so can write legible letters that are easy to read. People are asking us to join protests in various parts of the UK to stop fish farms, habitat destruction, and the demolition of an old building. The most interesting one is a letter asking us to come along to the opening of an urban park, where local people have created an area with bushes, flowers, and small trees in the middle of a city, so that local wildlife has somewhere to live with various food options for different types of creatures. There is even a small pond for ducks and other small waterfowl. This is the kind of celebration we want to advertise, as this is a success story and something to give hope for the future. We put this letter at the top of the pile.

We decide to have a snack for lunch and then a nap before trying to open the second set of letters.

I awake to Gemma tapping me on the nose with her right front paw. She's always been better at disciplined sleeping than me and doesn't seem to need an alarm. The second set of letters bound with a red elastic band awaits. This time Gemma has a technique to fillet the band, and it doesn't last long. Gemma manages to slit open fifteen letters, whereas I only open three. My paw-eye coordination is obviously lacking, as

I tend to tear the envelope to shreds rather than surgically slitting it open with a single claw, like Gemma does. Anyway, we read the letters together. Strangely, most of these letters are in cursive writing and more difficult to read as a result. The seventh letter isn't difficult to read though – it simply says WE KNOW WHERE YOU LIVE in blue ink.

Gemma looks at the envelope and sees that the postmark is clear.

"That's a silly thing to write, isn't it?" she says. "They got the address correct, so why leave a message inside an envelope telling us something we are already aware of by looking at the outside of the envelope?"

"I think it's meant to be threatening," I say, "but the envelope is postmarked and the stamp is franked, so it wasn't hand delivered but sent via the mail system, so what they're really saying is that they know our address and are able to write the address on an envelope and have the postal service handle it correctly and deliver it on time. I doubt they've been to the house. The postmark is from Wales, somewhere in North Wales. We should keep those two items together. Perhaps the humans might want to contact the police about this, although it could be pranksters."

"There are some odd people about, aren't there?" says Gemma. "Now this letter is more interesting. We've been invited to a children's protest about the building of an incinerator near a school – how ridiculous is that?"

"Is the date on a weekend?" I ask. "If it isn't, we might not be able to go, as Mary and John will be at work and won't be able to escort us there."

"We need a calendar, don't we?" says Gemma, "so we can send meaningful replies to people, saying we rely on humans to transport us to places."

"Most people are giving their email addresses, so that's a good thing, and perhaps if we can't attend, we can still send a goodwill message wishing them every success with their event," I say.

"Yes, we can write a message 'Good Luck with your event' where each of the words is on a separate piece of paper and if we use ten different coloured crayons, we can have ten different goods, ten different lucks etc and give each event a distinct message rather than a generic message written in black ink."

"Yes, we can do that. That PC of yours has a camera, doesn't it?"

"It does, and I think I can record items and edit them, so a unique message for each event is definitely possible."

Then I remember something: "Do you know where Mary's travel laptop is?"

"I do. It's in her desk downstairs, which I can paw open from underneath. Why do you ask?"

"Well, Rufus says he wants to start writing poetry, and I said we might be able to lend him a laptop to use."

"The squirrel? The squirrel writes poetry?" Gemma looks stunned. "Can he type?"

"I don't think Rufus can type, but he could dictate it to me, and I could type it in."

"That might be better. Your paws are small, neat, and clean, whereas his paws are filthy and large. But wait, I could use an oddball character for my book. A squirrel who writes poetry might fit the bill."

"Squirrels aren't pets," I say.

"Alright, another rodent that writes poems, a rat or a hamster."

"How about a mouse who writes an Ode to Robert Burns? The mouse is apologising for chewing a book of Burns's poetry to make a house?"

"That's a good idea, and mice are acceptable pets, aren't they?"

"Yes, I suppose so, but the pet shop owner wouldn't make much profit from selling mice unless he sold them in bulk."

"That is true, but shops do stock certain items called loss leaders, where they don't expect to make money from them, but those stocks entice people into the shop, so they purchase other items with more of a mark-up on them."

"So, we could let Rufus write his poetry indirectly," I say, "as long as we can use Mary's laptop?"

"Well, you use John's laptop to write your diary thing," says Gemma, "so you could use that for Rufus, too."

"That is true, well that's good. At least we can provide options for Rufus, but I was thinking that Mary's laptop is more portable, and we could use it on the window ledge, so Rufus doesn't walk through the house. You mentioned his claws were filthy."

"Yes, that's true. I'll paw open her drawer, grab the laptop, and carry it upstairs in my mouth. And return it the same way."

"I'm not sure how often he'll want to write poetry," I say, "so we'll see how things turn out."

We carry on reading the letters sent to us and are greatly amused by some of them. Once we finish, Gemma is really excited about all the things she has to do and so she goes downstairs to write a to-do list, so she won't forget anything. There are some crayons and a packet of printer paper for use with the computer, so Gemma will also figure out how to produce multi-coloured messages for people and their events. I decide to read some more of *The Card* underneath the couch.

At about 5:50pm, Gemma scurries into the lounge.

"We're going to need Mary and John's help with sending messages to people. I can't write cursive handwriting using those crayons, they're too smooth and I can't grip them. That means I can't write messages in many colours with crayon."

"I see," I reply. "Can you get the crayons and the paper and put them on the table here? Perhaps this is another opportunity for us to use our ESP skills?"

"Oh, good idea. Transmit thoughts of writing with crayons on pieces of paper?"

"Yes, particularly if we place the letters next to the crayons and paper on the table and gaze appealingly at them."

"I'll get the crayons. They're in a small holder, so I can carry them. The paper will be trickier to carry, as I might wet the paper with my mouth."

"Put the paper in a magazine and carry the magazine?" I suggest.

Gemma scoots away and soon returns with the paper in a health and wellness magazine. She plonks this on the table and returns downstairs for the crayons. I separate the paper from the magazine and hide the magazine under the TV stand, as I don't want it to be a distraction.

I paw the paper into something approaching a neat pile and Gemma puts the crayons on top of the paper, but slightly to one side. We both grab some letters in our mouths and put them on the table next to the crayons. It looks like a presentable scene. Finally, Gemma carries a spare blue crayon in her mouth from downstairs and puts that on top of the pile of letters.

"Now all we do is transmit thoughts about writing in different colours on the paper," I say.

"It's that easy, is it?" says Gemma.

"When they've seen the writing materials, the paper, and the fan mail, they'll be more receptive to the ideas that we send via our thoughts," I say, "they must be on the right wavelength to receive our thoughts."

"I see," says Gemma. I detect a hint of scepticism in these two words, but this is no time for negative thoughts from the Freddie cat, so I ignore them.

We sit on the table and face the front door with all the items in front of us. We don't normally sit on the table and face the front door, so hopefully this will attract their attention.

A key is inserted into the front door and Mary comes in, carrying her work bag in her left hand. She slips off her shoes and walks through to the kitchen, casting a glance in our direction, and saying, "Hello, kitties." This is not a promising start, but I am determined to stay positive.

I hear the kettle filled and switched on, then the sound of rummaging in the cupboard for some tea, probably a nice Earl Grey as a reward for working hard all day. I have never drunk tea myself as it's normally too hot, but some of them do smell quite lovely.

Mary's head appears around the kitchen doorway.

"Why are you two sitting on the table?" she asks.

"Oh, she has noticed," says Gemma with a lot of irony.

"You two never sit on the table. What are you up to?"

I paw at the crayon and Gemma taps on the letters.

"Wait a sec, kitties," says Mary and goes back into the kitchen, reappearing a few seconds later with a hot tea.

"Do we start the thought transfers now?" asks Gemma.

"Yes, Gemma, writing, colours, paper, crayons, good luck messages, that sort of thing."

"What do we have here?" says Mary, "...oh, the letters have started in earnest, haven't they...?" She looks at a few of them and reads two or three, "Well, Freddie and Gemma, we can't take you to all these places, but this one..." she brandishes a letter "...we can take you to I suppose, it's an hour from here, and it's on a Saturday."

Mary looks at another of the letters and then says: "So, kitties, what's the idea behind the crayons and paper? Do you want to write to them? Or send them a message?"

I miaow, as this is getting close to what we want. I'm not sure how we would convey the word video, other than perhaps holding a piece of paper between us and pointing at the TV?

"Oh, what's this..." says Mary, "we know where you

live… and you've kept the envelope with the letter, well done, we'll have to contact the police about this…"

At this moment, the front door opens, and John comes in. Mary waits for him to deposit his work things before asking him to come over to the table. Both Gemma and I tilt our heads slightly and look at him hopefully. He picks up the envelopes near the front door and waves them at us.

"You kitties have been busy, haven't you? I can tell which ones Gemma opened and which ones you opened, Freddie. Gemma has much sharper claws, and hers were opened with a single surgical slice, whereas yours aren't in a straight line and have been ripped open. Still, I have a feeling you'll be getting plenty of practice over the next few days as there's a lot of people talking about your tree saving."

As usual, Gemma tries to look modest and fails, but she licks her right-front paw by way of acknowledgement of the remarks.

"Look at this," says Mary, pushing the letter with 'We Know Where You Live' written on it.

John shakes his head sadly. "There's always someone who wants to spoil things… so I wouldn't worry too much about it, but how would the person writing that think it would mean anything to the cats?"

"I think the cats want to reply to these letters by writing messages, hence the paper and the crayons, and I was looking at the requests for personal appearances and we might be able to take them to one or two of them, but not all of them, as some are hundreds of miles away."

"Let's discuss it after we've had something to eat, there's

going to be a lot more of these requests, so perhaps we have to record a few videos with different messages or different coloured messages, hence the crayons, and then send them off via email."

As Mary and John head into the kitchen for their tea, taking the letters and envelopes with them, I have a disturbing thought. "Even though that message was in an envelope addressed to us, what if it was aimed at Mary and John, their names weren't mentioned in the news report, but whoever sent the message knew it would go to the right address if they addressed the letter to you and me."

Gemma eyes me sharply: "That's not a good thought, yes what if it is aimed at them? I'm not sure what we can do. On a positive note, John did notice the thought about sending via video, so hopefully we can do that soon."

Mary and John have tea together at the kitchen table rather than in front of the television and seem to be reading each of the letters carefully.

That evening, we are very busy. Mary and John write the words 'good' and 'luck' on one piece of paper, 'with' and 'your' on another piece of paper and the words 'event', 'protest', and 'demo' on separate pieces of paper with various combinations of coloured crayons. They then video us with the first two pieces of paper in front of us and add the 'event', 'protest', and 'demo' paper depending on who we are sending the message to. Mary keeps a list of the email addresses and an index of what each video says, plus the colours used, and to whom it has been sent. This is very organised. Mary and John also contact two people who we might be able to visit on the two upcoming weekends and attend their event, including the urban park idea.

We thank Mary and John by letting them stroke us for a few minutes and Gemma even purrs for a few seconds by way of gratitude. It sounds like our weekends will be full until we all leave to go to the Netherlands. And this is after just one day's worth of letters.

I fall asleep on the couch and have an unusual dream about sitting under a waterfall. The water suddenly turns into letters that flood over me. Then a giant red crayon starts chasing me through some trees and I have to grab a piece of paper saying 'Stop Chasing Me' on it before it goes away. As you can imagine, this was not a restful sleep.

Chapter 10

Today

THIS MORNING, AFTER MY BREAKFAST, I decide to visit Holly. She seems to be running well in her wheel, and I head over there after greeting the crows, starlings, and wasps who meet me in the front garden after I climb down the trellis. They tell me that Oliver hasn't left the house since the catnapping attempt, and this makes me sad. Iver likes going to the park. I tell them I'll meet them by our front garden gate at 10:45am so I can pay him a visit and find out what we can work out in terms of Oliver going in the park under observation by the birds and wasps. I must be back under the letterbox by noon to discover what the post lady brings in terms of requests for our presence. I am keen to find out who will summon us today.

I wave to Holly and then scamper across the garden, jump onto the fence, and scoot to her slightly open window.

"Hello, Holly, how are you?"

"Freddie… how are you?" says Holly. "I'm well, thank you. I've heard my human parents talking about you and Gemma, and another cat called Oliver. You helped save a tree in the park?"

"I'm fine too," I say. "Yes, we did, and it was thanks to the crows, starlings, finches, wasps, cats, and a squirrel."

"Yes, it was a joint effort by the sound of it," says Holly, coming to a halt for a rest.

"What have you been up to, Holly?" I ask.

"Well, when my owners don't lock my cage I scramble out and read one of the books on the shelf. They seem to have brought all the geography books up here and I can read them and dream about all the countries I'll never visit, at least not in this life."

"Oh, Holly, that's sad, isn't it? There's lots you can glean from reading books though, at least you can read the books and admire pictures of the places you want to visit, rather than never knowing what a place looks like."

"Yes, that's right, that's a very positive way of looking at it."

"And how much exercise are you doing? Are you reducing your running?"

"I am, I've reduced my exercise by about twenty-five percent, but reading those books gives me some mental exercise which I wasn't doing before, so I'm trying to keep a healthy mind in a healthy body."

"Mens sana in corpore sano," I say. "It's a good idea. I try to follow that rule, but I don't do as much exercise as you do."

"You can access books, can't you? Your human parents own a lot of books."

"They do and they keep buying new ones and putting them on the shelf so I can find them. Interestingly, they don't own too many geographical books, not like you have…books from every continent, Holly."

"I know, I'm lucky to have about twenty-five books about the real world."

"Yes, my book choices are mostly fiction," I reply, "and so I won't possess as rounded a view of the world as you do."

"You've been to the Netherlands though, to Amsterdam, so you must know more about the world than me."

"Only about Amsterdam. You know more about Egypt, Morocco, Iran, and lots of other places."

"And Syria," says Holly, "that's where my family is from, going back a lot of hamster generations, of course."

"Right. Have you seen anyone taking an interest in our house since I last spoke to you? I was referring to the man who was watching the house when we were all away, if you remember him. Particularly last Saturday?"

"I remember someone who was walking up and down outside your house when your human parents were being interviewed on the doorstep. I don't reckon it was the same person, although I might be wrong because the man monitoring the house when you were away never got out of his car."

"I see," I say, "well that's okay, I suppose. I should go. I must visit young Oliver the cat and encourage him to go out into the park."

"Why doesn't he want to go out?"

"Three men tried to catnap him, but they failed, mainly because of Wilf, who attacked the man who was guarding his garden gate and so Oliver could get back inside to safety."

"Perhaps Oliver needs protection of some kind?"

"He does, you're correct, but he shouldn't feel as though he's being given a bodyguard whenever he goes outside, as though he can't be independent and go out on his own. He just needs to know there's someone there for him if he needs help."

"Like a panic button?"

"Yes, something like that, but it's better not to refer to the word panic."

"A bell then?"

"Yes, something like that would be good," I say.

"I hope that helps, anyway I should start running again, so I can have a reading break in about thirty minutes."

"Yes, I'll be off. I'll speak to you soon. Take care."

"'Bye, Freddie, see you soon."

I wave au revoir and decide to be decisive and run around the fence for a bit of exercise.

I meet the birds and wasps as agreed and we head over to the park and towards Oliver's house. We don't observe any humans loitering with intent to catnap, so we head up the garden path and stop outside Oliver's front door.

"Oliver," I say through the cat flap, "are you there?"

There is a sound of claws on wood, and Oliver pokes his head through the flap.

"Oliver!" say the crows, starlings, and wasps.

"Hello," says Oliver, stepping outside, "are you going over to the park? Can I come too?"

"Yes," I say, "let's go. We should saunter around the park and show you there's nothing to fear. There are quite a few people around, so everything will be fine."

"Let's go then," says Oliver. "I'm needing a walk to stretch my legs." He scurries down his path and we all follow him gladly towards the green space on the other side of the road.

We parade around and come to a halt at a park bench, where we discuss how we can help Oliver feel more secure in the park. Oliver says he needs an early warning system, so the wasps volunteer to help him by scouting the park before Oliver steps out of his garden gate and to let him know how things are. The crows and starlings say they'll help too when Oliver is in the park and make sure that he always has a few friends close at hand. I, Freddie cat, will also accompany him whenever I am in the park.

With that settled, we enjoy the light breeze, the warm temperatures, and the lovely view of the trees for a few minutes before heading back to the playground where Rufus doesn't seem to be making much progress with the yellow swing. Indeed, he seems to be getting rather upset about it, which is making things worse, in my opinion.

"Try the slide," I suggest, "by way of a change. It'll do you good and you'll probably do well as you won't be overthinking your movements."

Rufus looks at me glumly, nods, and decides he'll try the slide.

Well, he really flies off the end and goes about two feet further than he's ever done before. He lands on his feet too after doing a somersault and receives everyone's congratulations.

"I'll leave it at that," he says. "I doubt I'll be able to beat that again today." He's really cheered up, and it is amazing to observe how one successful jump can make him so much happier. Oliver has a go at jumping on the yellow swing and the second time, he manages to get a really good swing going. He is joined by three crows and two finches who all land at the same time as the swing starts to descend and add some impetus. Oliver is really miaowing aloud, and it is wonderful. He's so happy.

I decide I should head back home. I wave goodbye to everyone for now and leave them in the playground. Seb, Rob, Andrea, and the wasps come with me to make sure I am okay.

"Wait a minute," says Seb, "there's a car there with two men sitting in it. I don't recognise them. Do you know them, Andrea and Rob?"

"No," say Rob and Andrea in unison.

"We see them," choruses Wilf, "and we'll monitor them. If they make a move, we'll intercept them. Please cross the road safely, Freddie cat."

I scoot down to the road and look carefully both ways before crossing. The crows squawk a farewell. I watch the car with the men in it, but they've not moved. Wilf has formed a large arrow above the car, so there is no doubt about which car is being monitored. I wave to the wasps, and they move back to the playground.

=========

Gemma is already in position under the letter box when I arrive back at the house. She looks pleased and her tail is still, indicating a certain inner peace.

"How did the writing go this morning?" I ask.

"It went well. The rabbit is in the middle of writing his first email to the police, as dictated by the budgie, outlining what they discovered on their first night patrol outside the pet shop."

"That sounds exciting," I say. "What did they find?"

"A robbery at a shop and they also found a body in the cemetery, draped over a gravestone, but they didn't mention that part to the police. They found out the identity of the person and some other clues, but they haven't been able to follow up on those items yet."

"Because they must be back in the shop before opening time?" I say.

"That's correct, and they can only do a bit of research on the Internet before the owner of the shop arrives."

"It's all worked out in your head by the sounds of it," I say.

"In real life, I also checked the email that Mary and John set up for us last night," says Gemma, "and we received eight replies thanking us for our videos. We're making a difference already. Oh, and the representatives of Agatha replied, saying that the title of *Cat Amongst the Pigeons* was meant to be metaphorical rather than an indication of the contents of the book."

"That's not very satisfying," I reply. "How are we supposed to know whether a title is metaphorical as opposed to describing the contents of the book?"

"I asked Agatha's people that same question, but I don't believe they'll reply, somehow. I reckon they believed I wasn't a cat, just a human pretending to be a cat."

"On the other hand, it's good we received so many replies so quickly. I wonder how many letters we'll get today?"

"More than yesterday, I'd say about forty, and hopefully not bound together with elastic bands. I really don't like elastic bands."

"You're good at shredding them," I say, and Gemma flexes her claws in a rather overt way.

"Are you going to read me some of your story?" I continue.

"Of course, after we've looked at the letters that come today. I'll read you the part where the pets find the body in the cemetery."

"That sounds exciting," I say. "I've never been in a graveyard before."

"Me neither," says Gemma, "but I've seen pictures, and it looks a bit odd really, but humans do strange things sometimes."

"The post lady might be here," I say. "I can hear someone coming along the path."

Gemma and I stare up at the letterbox and it seems to take hours before the letters come pouring through. No elastic bands today. We both step back, otherwise letters would land on us, a bit like my dream the previous night, which is a bit scary as that's the first time I can remember a dream being predictive. But without the water, thankfully.

The fall of letters stops, and we stare around us. There must be seventy letters. We both start pawing them into small piles of ten. There are two letters for Mary and John as well as ours, so we put those to one side. We both start opening letters and reading the contents. The few I read are mainly inviting Gemma and I to children's birthday parties and other household events, not environmental protests or demonstrations. I place party invitations into a separate pile from the few environment-related letters we receive.

"Are you placing the letters into separate piles depending on the nature of the request?"

"That's a great idea, Fred. I'll do that now. What are you getting requests about?"

"Children's parties, mostly," I reply.

"Yes, same here." Gemma is beginning to flick her tail around, as though she is finding this task irritating.

We continue our appraisal of the letters, and this takes nearly two hours in total. When we collate our piles, there are fifty-six invitations to children's parties or events, five to environmental protests, six to demonstrations, two to cookery demonstrations, and three to barbecues.

"This is a bit disappointing," I say. "I was hoping for more environmental events to go to, or at least be invited to. What about you?"

"I'm not sure how we should reply to birthday party invitations, because we should be polite and yet discouraging. If we attended one children's party, we'd receive even more invitations. We shouldn't spread ourselves too thinly and we should concentrate on environmental protests, as you suggested."

"This invitation sounds interesting," I say, "it says: Dear Gemma and Freddie, it was inspiring to watch you on the television supporting the trees in your park. Would you come to our demonstration against a tree felling in our local park a week on Saturday? We hope you can come as it's not that far from your place to here. I suppose your humans would drive you. I like how Gemma glared at the camera all the time and how Freddie seemed to be smiling all the time. Yours sincerely, Wendy the Siamese Cat."

"A female cat?" says Gemma, "and a Siamese too. One of my main characters is a Siamese cat, although she's called Bridget. They're supposed to be clever, even for cats."

"They're moody though, and like showing off."

"You should put that letter at the top of the pile, because if I can observe Wendy's behaviour, then it will make my characterisation of Bridget more accurate."

"Okay, will do. Did you read a letter you prefer to all the others?"

"Yes, actually, I do. Now you come to mention it. This one is from Alan: Hello, Gemma and Freddie, I liked your protest technique, and I hope you can come here and help us. The local council wants to dig up our local green space and build a swimming pool on the land, even though there is a lake a mile away and a river nearby. If they looked after the river and lake better, then people would swim there. Can you help us? And then it's signed by Alan and someone else, whose name looks like Alsatian. I don't believe it's a dog's signature, and the letter doesn't smell of dog, thankfully."

"A swimming pool isn't as nice as a river or lake," I say. "The council should encourage exercise in nature and not inside buildings all the time."

"Indeed, so let's put those two letters at the top of the pile and find out what the humans say."

I am feeling parched, so I go into the kitchen and lap at the cold tap, which has developed a drip in recent days. I say hello to the primroses and the cacti, who are enjoying the warmth on the windowsill.

"Freddie," says Gemma, appearing at the top of the stairs, "I can read you some of my book, if you'd like."

"Yes," I say, jumping to the floor, "let's go and I'll listen."

Gemma scoots downstairs and I follow her. She lies down in front of her computer and once I indicate I am ready to listen, she starts to read.

"The scene is that Bridget the Siamese cat, Vera the black cat, Emily the budgie, Ashley the rabbit, and Wendell the parrot have exited the pet shop via the cat flap and are walking down the pavement in the small town of Newton Oaks. It's about one o'clock in the morning…

As the pets walked along next to the wall, they all heard a crash, like the breaking of glass, the noise coming from the opposite side of the road in the vicinity of Willetts, the greengrocers. Sure enough, around twenty seconds later, someone unlocked the door from inside and ran out carrying a bag and headed away towards St Matthew's Church.

"A man robbed the shop," says Emily.

"He broke the glass in the side window and went in through that and came out of the front door a few seconds later," says Vera.

"He couldn't have taken much," observes Bridget, "as he wasn't in there too long, only a few seconds at most."

Emily and Wendell flew after the robber as the cats and rabbit scampered towards the church, heading into the churchyard. The rows of tombstones looked irregular as the clouds kept obscuring the moon.

"Oh, look," says Ashley, "that grave over there seems strangely misaligned compared to the others."

"Let's go and investigate," says Vera.

The pets padded over towards the oddly shaped stone. It soon became apparent what was causing the oddness. A human body was slumped on the top of a grave. Blood was evident on the side of their head, as though the human had tripped and landed on the stone. Emily and Wendell landed on a nearby cross.

"We followed the robber," says Wendell, "and we know who it is, don't we, Em?"

"Yes, it's the lady who lives on Elm Lane with a white door and extravagant black hinges. I think it's number twenty-three."

"That's Mrs Peebles," says Bridget, "but I thought she walked with a limp. That robber didn't have a limp. He or she was quite fit."

"I think she's taken in a lodger recently," says Vera, "a younger man who works in the garage in the town."

"Well, that's one thing sort of solved," says Ashley, "but who is this in front of us?"

"The man with the knife in his back?" says Wendell.

"Knife?" says Bridget, Vera, and Ashley simultaneously.

"A carving knife," says Emily, "we get a better view from up here."

"So, it's not an accident then," says Bridget, "does anyone recognise him?"

"He looks like the postman. What's his name, Mr James?" says Wendell.

"Oh yes, it is," says Emily, "he's got the skin blemish by his left eye, a liver spot I think they're called by humans, even though they're nothing to do with the liver, but caused by excessive exposure to the sun."

"What's he doing out so late?" asks Vera. "Surely he would have to get up really early to do his round?"

Gemma stops reading at that point and looks at me for a reaction.

"Well," I say, "it certainly zips along at a good pace, and I like how you wrote a number of different perspectives, from the birds' perspective and from the cats' and rabbit's perspective, so there's two different views being described."

Gemma's tail begins to move, almost imperceptibly, up and down.

"The one thing you should be aware of is that in the pitch black of night, a budgerigar might not be able to identify a liver spot on a human face from a cross. I'm not sure that a budgerigar's eyesight is that good."

Gemma's tail stops.

"That's a good point, I'd missed that. It's night, of course it is."

"You need some sound in the churchyard too, though not a cliched sound like an owl or a badger, and perhaps you could describe the wind blowing through the trees, ruffling the birds' feathers or the rabbit's fur."

"Yes, that's a good idea. Some movement would be good, just slight movement, nothing major."

"Is this the start of the book? Have the characters been described already?"

"They've been described already, but I understand what you mean about adding in small details about the characters now and then."

"That's everything for now," I say. "Is it going to be one long story or many short stories?"

"Well, I'll see. It might be better to start with shorter stories and then work up to something longer."

"That sounds like a good idea. The rabbit, Ashley, will write the emails to the police as dictated by Emily. Is that right?"

"Yes, that's correct, the rabbit Ashley is an excellent typist."

"That's good. Is there anything else we should discuss? If not, then I'll meet you upstairs at just before six, when Mary and John come home."

"Thank you. I'll make some changes based on your suggestions." Gemma starts to type some updates, and I head upstairs to read my latest book by Graham Greene called *England Made Me*. I'm not really getting along with this book, but I will persevere in case it improves, hopefully by the main character disappearing for a few pages. The book is set in Sweden just before WWII and is an unusual choice for Graham, as he normally prefers places like Haiti, Cuba, and Istanbul. Or perhaps it's me that prefers to read about these places in books? I'll ponder that.

Just before 6pm Gemma comes upstairs and we arrange the letters on the table again, like we did the previous today, our favourites on the top and the birthday party letters in a separate pile. We both agree that we don't want to attend any parties either individually or separately.

To our surprise, John comes through the front door first. We both look at him hopefully when he approaches us.

"More letters than yesterday, kitties?" he says, before heading into his room. He soon comes back out wearing his house clothes and scratches us both on the top of our heads. Casting an eye on the letters, he picks up the small pile of environmental ones and looks through them.

"This top letter is your preferred choice, is it, kitties?" he says.

We both miaow in agreement.

"It's not that far away from here, actually," says John.

We miaow as this is good to hear, even though we thought this was the case. Gemma had looked up the place in the car atlas, that's not in the car, and said that it was quite close in geographical terms, about two paw widths away is how she described it.

John picks up the next letter and reads it.

"This is your second choice, is it?" he says, gesturing to the letter.

We miaow again.

"They sort of answer you, don't they?" says Mary, who's come in through the back door from the garage, as she's driven to work today. She is wearing her black jumper and jeans, her standard evening attire.

"They do, but I'm not sure if they want to go to all the places in this pile..." and he taps the list of invitations to events, "...or they want to go to these events in this pile."

"Judging from Gemma's expression and the fact she's sitting on the thicker pile, we can assume they don't want to go to those events they've been invited to," says Mary. Gemma glares at John and starts to wag her tail.

"Looks like you're correct," says John. "What about this letter?" He picks up the third letter from the smaller pile. We stay silent. In unison.

"Just these first two," John continues, handing them to Mary.

"He's getting the idea," says Gemma, "and we should keep them happy, otherwise they might not drive us anywhere."

"I wonder when they're going to talk to us about going to Amsterdam?" I say.

"Well, I found their letter," says Gemma, "and it didn't mention we're going with them, so perhaps the intention is to tell them closer to the time?"

"Oh, I thought they'd be told straight away, so we should watch out for another letter from the Netherlands."

"It looks as though we should," says Gemma, "I hope they're not intending to keep us apart the whole time or even for us to go on a different train, so Mary and John aren't aware we've been away for the weekend."

"That wouldn't be good, would it?" I say.

John and Mary come over to us having had a discussion in the background.

"Kitties," says Mary, "there are a lot of people who would like to meet you, but we can't take you everywhere. You've provided us with four letters already and we can take you to these places over the next two weekends on day trips, as the events are happening on Saturdays and Sundays."

We miaow as this is good news.

"Then after those two weekends are over, we're all going away to the Netherlands, although you'll be travelling separately from us, as you must go through a quarantine check on the train. You will attend a special environmental gathering at Europoort while we're at the Van Gogh Museum and then we're all going to a gala event at the Rijksmuseum."

We look at each other as it sounds as though everything has been sorted out already, but we've not seen a letter.

"Someone must have phoned them," says Gemma, and I think she is right about that.

What this did mean was that over the next two and a half weeks, we had an interesting time of it. A significant event was that two yellow flowerpots appeared one day and were soon occupied by primroses. On weekdays, I went outside in the morning and Gemma wrote more of her novel before we met under the letter box and then sifted through all the post in the afternoon and sent emails and videos in the evening. The volume of post did increase especially after we were featured on the news when we visited environmental protests at the weekends, so people could see that writing to us did produce results. It did mean that not all our mail was pushed through the door. Sometimes a small bag was left outside on the doormat full of letters, quite often with incomplete addresses such as "Freddie and Gemma, England". All this activity did mean that I was unable to write many diary entries during this period and those I did write looked like the previous day's entries, so I deleted them as they weren't sufficiently different. I will recommence my diary on the day before we go away to the Netherlands.

Chapter 11

Today

THIS MORNING GEMMA AND I are excited as soon we'll be leaving to go back to the Netherlands. Mary and John have both gone to work early, so they can leave earlier than normal to catch the train under The Channel and then on to Brussels and Amsterdam. We will be going on the same train but travelling in a different compartment with Mrs Elkins. We will all be staying at Miep's house and Gemma reminds me that we must act as though we don't know where anything is, otherwise, Mary and John might be suspicious.

I decide to visit the library this morning as I want to find some pictures of Europoort near Rotterdam, and discover what landmarks there are, other than the tall Euromast. I prefer to find pictures in a book rather than on the Internet. Call me old-fashioned if you like, but that's my preference. There's a tactile satisfaction with reading a book that I don't experience when staring at a screen.

I soon find myself weighing up the best path to follow along the vine towards the librarian's window. This is like old times, even though it's only a few months since I was here last. I say 'hello' to the vine and the leaves rustle a greeting to me as I gingerly progress up the vine towards the window.

The window hasn't been cleaned since I was here last, by all appearances. The same spiders are still in residence. I'm glad it's open so I can peer inside and observe Angela, who's working on her computer. She is concentrating on entering some figures and is tracing them on a piece of paper with a finger on her right hand, while tapping the keyboard with a finger on her left hand. Angela's forehead is creased, and I decide not to interrupt until her face is smooth again. I crease my face too when I'm tapping away on the keyboard. It's just that no one can see the undulations under my fur. Fur is useful sometimes, though not as useful as whiskers for measuring distances. At least that's what I read about why I have whiskers.

"Phew," says Angela after a further two minutes and leans back in her chair. She looks happy, so I reckon it is a good time to miaow. I miaow.

"Freddie," she says, "how are you? Come down, Fred cat."

I'm pleased that Angela is pleased to see me. It's good we're both pleased. I jump down and walk across the carpet tiles to Angela. She picks me up and gives me a rub before placing me on her desk.

"You're popular, Freddie, you and Gemma. You're on the news and you're popular with people who attend events."

I miaow, this is true, but what concerns me is that we appear to be the story rather than the event we're attending. The event should be the story, the possible chopping down of the tree or the digging up of the green space should be the story. Although, according to Mary and John, when we say that we'll attend an event, the environmental reason for the event is either delayed or goes away completely. All of a sudden, the swimming pool doesn't have to be built in the park, or the tree gets a stay of execution.

"How can I help you, Fred?" asks Angela.

I stare at the keyboard and touch it with my paw.

"You can type something in. I'll give you a blank document to use."

This is a good idea as I don't want to write 'Europoort' all over Angela's figures in her report and cause her to have a furrowed brow again.

I type in Europoort but there's an autocorrect in the software and it makes the word Europort, but I add the extra 'O' again and the software accepts this but puts a red line under Europoort as it is still of the opinion I can't spell properly. But I know differently.

Angela looks at me and says, "What's that?"

I type in 'port', 'Rotterdam', and 'pictures'.

Angela types in some search items on the library system and then heads out of her office, presumably to fetch a book of pictures of Europoort. According to the list, there are two books in the business section and one in the transport section, with a subsection of trade.

Angela is away for about two minutes and then returns clutching three books, two of which are what I would call coffee table books. She puts them down on the desk to her left and opens the largest of the books. I position myself so that I can hold down one side of the book with my left-front paw and page through the book with my right-front paw. I put both my back paws on the bottom of the book to hold it down.

I start paging through and there are plenty of pictures of the port facilities and hundreds of containers. Indeed, Europoort handles twelve million containers a year, and that seems like a lot to me. There are many tens of storage containers for oil and warehouses, cranes, and everything seems vast. I marvel at how Cornelius will find the correct ship out of all the ones there could be in the port.

At that moment, Angela's colleague, Roger, comes into the room and examines me closely. I have to say he doesn't appreciate cats as much as Angela does.

"Angela, there's a cat on your desk leafing through a book on shipping. What's it doing?"

"Roger, it's your friend Fred, and he's come into the office and he's leafing through a book on shipping, as you say. He's looking for pictures of Europoort, the port of Rotterdam on the Rhine and Meuse."

"Why would a cat be interested in one of the world's biggest port facilities?"

"Cats are curious creatures, Roger, and perhaps he's interested in where his cat litter comes from or where his cat food comes from?"

"Angela, he seems more interested in the layout of the port than anything else, a view he'd only get from above, if you understand what I mean."

Angela shakes her head and glances at me with a look of pity on her face. I close my eyes slowly and open them again, to show that I agree with her sadness regarding Roger's stereotyping of cats.

Angela looks at Roger: "Are you suggesting he's somehow going to be seeing the Europoort from above, as though he's going to be on a broomstick with a woman wearing a pointed hat sitting in front of him?"

"You're taking the mickey, Angela, that cat is up to no good, I can feel it. He's not looking at containers, cranes, and ships but the layout of the port."

"Away with you, Roger. Go and cause trouble somewhere else. How can a cat like Fred cause trouble? What's he going to do? Scratch a hole in a container with his claws?"

Roger glares at me and then leaves Angela's office. He's a silly man to imagine that I, Mr Freddie Cat, could be plotting to disrupt the trade at Europoort by looking at photos of the port.

I continue to paw through the pictures as Angela works on her spreadsheet of figures, which appear to be the gross and net expenditure on books per library department. The figures for Europoort are staggering as the place processes over thirty-two thousand containers per day, every day of the year.

I miaow when I finish the book, and Angela puts another book in front of me. There are more words than pictures in this one, however this second book does indicate how many ships there can be in Europoort at one time, and how many berths there are for these ships. I hope we're given some accurate information as to where our ship will moor, otherwise Cornelius's sense of smell will be severely tested.

About an hour later, when I complete the second and third

books, Angela takes them back to the shelves and I inspect the office, including the photocopier, which now holds no interest for me whatsoever. I've been through that phase and hopefully matured so that I never return to it again. Angela comes back and gives me a stroke and tells me that I'm a good cat. She says she has to go to a meeting now and perhaps I should go in case Roger comes back and tries to perform an exorcism.

I miaow as I agree I should go. I have to give myself a good wash before I go on that train with Gemma, Mrs Elkins, Mary, and John. Mary and John will be travelling in a different compartment to us on the same train. Gemma says they're travelling First Class and we're in steerage, but I'm pretty sure Gemma has confused the train with a luxury liner and that we'll be going under water rather than on top of it. Gemma can still be bolshie sometimes and I wonder whether one of the characters in her book will turn out to be extremely left wing. Perhaps a budgie could be clumsy, and Gemma could describe it as having two left wings and be a communist sympathiser as a result. This would be a play on words as clumsy humans are described as having two left feet, usually when they're dancing. John has two left feet in the morning when he's not dancing and wanders into things that he avoids later in the day.

==========

When I get back home, Gemma is having a snack as she's completed one of the short stories in her book. She says there will be four stories altogether and not all of them involve murder. There will be at least one mystery as to who stole a tea cosy from a washing line. This sounds like an inventive story as I'm not sure who would steal a tea cosy. Few people use teapots these days, although a kitten could curl up comfortably in a cosy. On the other hand, a kitten on a washing line sounds like an accident waiting to happen. I'm sure Gemma will sort things out and make them realistic.

She trots off and I go upstairs to have a wash and read The Card under the couch. Although Mary and John have done some packing already, they're likely to be dashing around when they get home and it's best not to get under their feet. Gemma and I are packed already, of course, as we travel light and just bring ourselves.

I finish my book. Edward Henry Machin, known as Denry Machin, is *The Card* of the title. He's known as Denry because his mother realised she could save a certain amount of time each and every day by calling him Denry instead of Edward Henry. The story is mostly set in The Five Towns apart from excursions to Llandudno and Switzerland. The Five Towns in Bennett's books are based on five towns in The Potteries, i.e. Stoke, Hanley, Tunstall, Longton, and Burslem. The names of Bennett's Five Towns are changed slightly from their actual names, so Burslem becomes Bursley and Hanley Hanbridge, for example. A sixth town, Fenton, is often added into The Potteries now, but in this book I don't believe it's referred to.

Denry Machin is a bit of a rogue and a wheeler and dealer who gets a leg up in life by changing his marks in a geography exam when no one is looking and so manages to receive a scholarship to a better school. However, Denry goes from the backstreets of Bursley to living in a large house based on business acumen and a great deal of calculated risk taking, as well as a few sly actions when no one is looking. However, what Denry does best is that he knows how to cheer people up, whether by buying a star striker with his own money for the local football team, or by setting up a Universal Thrift Club that is so successful that it would end up bankrupting him, if he didn't do something in the nick of time to prevent this happening. He has foresight and skill. The book is a joy to read and I'm now looking for the next Arnold Bennett book to read.

I decide to have a snooze and dream that I'm asleep in a tea cosy on a washing line in a backstreet town in Victorian times. All of a sudden, someone steals me and takes me to Crewe station where I'm put on a train to London. That's when I feel someone tickling my chin and I open my eyes to find Mrs Elkins smiling at me.

She whispers to me that she will be coming with us rather than staying at our home and looking after us like she did last time. She gives me a big wink, which I know means that I, Freddie cat, am part of a conspiracy where only certain information is shared. Apparently, we got on so well with Mrs Elkins last time that she seems like the ideal person to take care of us on a potentially stressful train journey! WINK! Her friend Mrs Wilkins will house sit for the whole weekend and two men both called Mr Smith will monitor the house from outside, just to make sure that everything is well. The house will be more secure than when we're at home.

I stretch and go downstairs to have a final snack, drink,

and poo before heading out. I return upstairs to find Gemma carefully inspecting her cat carrier as though she's never seen it before. I remember to do the same as cats never like going into enclosed spaces voluntarily the first they're shown them by humans – there's a degree of suspicion and a cat will only enter on its own terms after all possibilities have been weighed up and considered. This can sometimes take many months and frustrate humans as a result. I peer inside my carrier and discover my favourite blue blanket. This is appealing, and I glance at Gemma, who is now on top of her carrier, testing the outside with her paw.

"It's time to go," I say. "We don't want to miss the train."

"Yes, you're right," says Gemma, and jumps down from her carrier and scurries inside.

I miaow at Mary, John, and Mrs Elkins and amble nonchalantly into my carrier. I use my claws to feel the softness of the blanket and start to purr. We're off on another adventure.

==========

Gemma and I are carried onto the train and taken into a compartment with Mrs Elkins. Our carriers are placed on a table facing inwards. There is no one else in the compartment. Mrs Elkins puts a cup of water in my carrier, and I miaow my thanks. Gemma receives a cup, too. Mrs Elkins leaves my carrier's door open, but I don't try to get outside as I'm not sure what is going to happen. Mrs Elkins will accompany us all the way to Amsterdam rather than handing us over in Brussels as happened last time. As the train starts off, there is a knock and a woman in uniform comes into the compartment.

"Are these the two cats?" she asks.

"Yes, these are the two, Freddie and Gemma," replies Mrs Elkins.

She peers into my carrier and gives me a gentle pat. I purr, and she rubs me gently.

"He seems healthy," she says, "and he's going to Amsterdam just for the weekend?"

"Yes, the two cats are integral to the dissolution of a people-smuggling operation in Rotterdam at Europoort."

"Right, and these are the two that gathered the information last year, followed those people?"

"That's right, and Gemma is in the other carrier."

The lady moves to inspect Gemma and strokes her, too.

"They seem to be happy and healthy animals. I hope they're as successful in their endeavours as last time." The lady smiles at me and leaves the compartment.

"Okay, Freddie and Gemma," says Mrs Elkins, "that's all. I'll turn you around so you can look out of the window. We're facing the opposite direction from the previous time, and you'll have a view of the other side of the tracks this time."

"We're travelling fast already," says Gemma. "I can barely see anything. What about you?"

"No, I can't see anything either, so I'm going to read my thin book, *The Crying of Lot 49* and maybe have a snooze."

"I'm missing my computer. I'd like to be writing some more of my book, but I'll just have to ponder some storylines for the animals in the pet shop. I really need one of those mobile devices so I can tap in my thoughts as they occur to me and they'll be recorded somewhere, whereas with thoughts they sometimes get lost, and I can't remember them."

The train speeds on and I read Mr Pynchon's book with some interest, but there is no real storyline as such, just a lot of zany characters with odd names. I am not enjoying it, and I don't regard it as satirical as the blurb on the cover indicates. Really, I shouldn't read the advertising but just read the book and then find out if I agree with the advertising afterwards.

We soon head under the Channel and come out the other side. I reckon Gemma is asleep, as I can hear her breathing steadily. Mrs Elkins gives me a treat and pours more water into my little bowl. She does the same with Gemma's bowl. There's a lot of activity when we get to Lille. This station is a high-speed train hub in Northern France where you can change from Eurostar onto a direct TGV high-speed train to Lyon, Avignon, Marseilles, Bordeaux, Brittany, Nîmes, and Montpellier. All those stations are mentioned in the announcements both inside and outside the train. These TGV trains bypass Paris, so there's a lot of planning involved to have such a fast and efficient train system. I'm not sure I'd want to fly to Marseilles, if I could get the train all the way, with just one change.

As we leave Lille and head for Brussels, we have a wonderful surprise. Miep comes into our carriage. Apparently, she had a security meeting near Lille and just so happens to have caught the same train as us. This is a good thing and I'm so pleased to see her, even though I have never officially 'met' her, of course. She gives me plenty of strokes and I purr loudly, as it's good to be with her. Gemma wakes up and extends a paw through her door so Miep can touch her. Then, we both sit in our carriers and face her as we both sense she has something to tell us, something important.

"Gemma and Freddie, I know you will understand me. It's no coincidence that I'm here. I have some updates for you because things have changed slightly. You'll still be going to Europoort tomorrow afternoon, but the ship we want you to investigate has been allocated a different berth than normal. It's slightly further from where the environmental protest will take place and you might have to walk further, although I think someone might give you two and the squirrels a lift on their bike. Cornelius will be on patrol from noon, and we'll arrange a rendezvous. Cornelius will walk close to the ship and see how many members of the crew there are before letting us know. He'll also try to work out where the people are being held. What we need you to do along with Bertie and Johann is to get onboard the ship and find the people, all the people, as we understand they'll be held in more than one cabin or hold. Johann can distract the crew if they get too nosey by throwing acorns at them. We've made him a small bag, like a rucksack, where he can store a few acorns and Bertie will be wearing one too, although his main role will be to untie any knots so that people can be easily released. Once you've found the people, you should come and tell us, so we can come onto the ship and prove that they're travelling against their will. That has to happen while they're on board. If the crew forces them on to the dockside, then we will find it difficult to prove those people came from one particular ship. The crew would argue those people were already there and hadn't come from the ship."

"How many crew do you expect there to be?" asked Mrs Elkins, a good question and one I would have asked if I could.

"Our understanding is that there will be twenty to twenty-two altogether," replies Miep, "and five of those are solely there to guard the people on board. They might well be armed in the port, but nothing ostentatious, perhaps sidearms or a knife."

I cringe when I hear that as it sounds dangerous and I don't fancy being shot at by anyone, let alone a people smuggler. On the other hand, an average-sized feline with stubby front legs creeping around a ship shouldn't engender a hail of bullets from anyone. Besides, gunfire might draw unwelcome attention from the port authorities, who might start asking questions as bullets and gas storage facilities won't mix well and big explosions could result.

Miep provides lots more information about who'll be involved and how many people from the security services will be undercover that day. This is good to hear, but they still won't be on the ship with us, and we will be at risk. Miep also says that we shouldn't be on the ship for long, perhaps forty-five minutes at most. It would largely depend on where the people are held.

There is quite a lot of information to process. Gemma seems quiet, too. I go back to reading my book, but I can't really understand the story and I fall asleep. I wake up when I am being carried off the train in Amsterdam.

Gemma and I are reunited with Mary and John. We all travel in the same vehicle to Miep's house. Mary and John get their own room and Gemma and I are in the same room as before, so everything is familiar, although we pretend not to know where everything is, at least for a few minutes. After I am let out of my carrier, I take the book *The Crying of Lot 49* in my mouth and place it on the bookshelf. I glance around the room and find a book called *A Third Class Murder,* with a representation of a train on the front. I manage to paw this book off the bookshelf and put it in my carrier for the journey back in three today's time. I like to plan ahead if at all possible. Gemma is eating a snack and using the litter tray, so you now know our different priorities.

Miep knocks on the door and says we were all going to meet outside in her front garden, so we can talk about what will happen on the following today. We scamper down the hallway, leap through the cat flap, and look around the garden. Nothing much has changed. Some birds on a branch wave their wings and a crow flaps down to sit on the grass next to us. The air is still and feels warm.

"Hello, Freddie and Gemma," says Henk, "how are you both?"

"I'm fine," I reply. "How are you, Henk?"

"I'm a bit tired from the journey," says Gemma, "but otherwise okay, it's good to be back."

"I'm fine too," says Henk, "and looking forward to working with you again tomorrow at the Europoort."

"Will there be many crows helping?" asks Gemma.

"We will have the full complement of crows around about. We have twelve for the whole of Europoort who watch and observe all the time, but tomorrow they'll be around your ship, plus the crows who are normally in Rotterdam will be there too, but further away watching all the routes to your ship of which there are many."

"It sounds very organised," I say, "and it seems we'll have a lot of support."

"It's taking quite a lot of organising, but we were only put on this trail by your work here last year when you followed those people, and we worked backwards from them."

"The cats have made friends already," says John, "even Gemma." He and Mary are looking around the garden and admiring the various items of garden furniture, including the white wooden chairs that Mary likes the look of as she is testing them out by sitting in them and then lifting them up to see how much they weigh.

"These are your human parents?" asks Henk.

"Yes, Mary and John, and they supposedly don't know anything about our trip here last year," says Gemma.

"Ouch," I say, "what was that?"

"Johann," says Henk, "just saying hello in his own style. He's up there on that branch."

"Yes, he's there along with the Bertie squirrel," Gemma informs me. "Johann doesn't appear to have any more nuts. I presume he's saving his throwing arm until tomorrow."

At that moment, Miep comes out of the house holding a large tray of appetisers and Mrs Elkins follows with a tray of drinks for the humans, plus a couple of bowls for the animals. Johann and Bertie soon materialise by the table and Bertie starts to eat the nut that Johann had thrown at me, hitting me on the backside.

"I hope you'll be as accurate tomorrow as you were just now," I say to Johann.

"Ah yes, Freddie cat, I will. Do you like the rucksack they have made for me?" says Johann, showing me a small bag that fits snugly under his belly, where he could stow three nuts.

"Oh, that's nice, and it matches your fur," says Gemma.

"Colour coordinated," says Johann, "an important consideration when going undercover. Bertie has one too, don't you Bertie?"

Bertie is chewing the nut, but nods and points to his bag.

"Does Bertie throw things too?" I ask.

"No, Freddie, he carries them for me, so I can have six nuts to throw, rather than just three. It could be very important, especially tomorrow."

While we've been talking about nuts and bags, the humans have been taking some food and drinks. After they've consumed some of their food, Miep hits a glass with a small spoon, which has the conditioned response that all the humans stop talking at exactly the same time. Bertie continues to eat his nut.

Miep speaks: "I'd like to welcome Mary and John, Gemma and Freddie, and Mrs Elkins from the UK to my home for the weekend. The time, I'm sure, will pass all too quickly, but let's enjoy our time together. Tomorrow, after a late breakfast and a walk around our neighbourhood, Mary and John will go to the Van Gogh Museum and have a special tour of the exhibition with an experienced guide who will show you around all the paintings the museum has managed to gather together from all over the world. Gemma and Freddie, we will take you to the demonstration at the Europoort, where I know they're looking forward to seeing you. Then in the evening, we'll all meet up at The Rijksmuseum for a wonderful celebration of their latest exhibition and Mary and John, you will be allowed to wheel around Gemma and Freddie on a tea trolley so they can enjoy the exhibition too."

"You've thought of everything," says Mary. "I'm so impressed."

"On Sunday, we have a special surprise lined up for all of you and obviously I'm not going to say what that is, but you will all enjoy it, I'm sure."

"I wonder what that will be?" says Gemma.

"Let's see, I have an idea, but I might be wrong," I reply.

Gemma gives me her quizzical look, but I stay stumm as I just want to get tomorrow out of the way. I am a bit worried as there seem to be a lot of crows involved, and that means a lot of observation is required to make sure we are all going to be alright. I meditate for a few seconds and try to get myself to live in the moment and let tomorrow take care of itself.

"Are you alright, Frederick?" asks Gemma.

"I'm fine," I say. "How about you?"

"I'm wondering," says Gemma, "I'm wondering where Mrs Elkins fits in to all this, and what her role is. I think she might be the UK equivalent of Miep in which case we should be honoured, but I'm wondering where she's going tomorrow. I would imagine she'll come to Europoort with us, but I wonder if that's it?"

"She will. I think the idea is to convince Mary and John, both directly and indirectly, that Mrs Elkins will look after us when we're apart from them."

"Yes, she's our minder, isn't she?" replies Gemma.

We continue our conversation with the squirrels and crows as the sun gradually falls down the sky, only to be replaced by some lovely Chinese lanterns that cast a reddish hue over the garden. The crows fly off and the squirrels head back to Vondelpark. Gemma and I head over to where Mary and John are holding hands and sit under their chairs and have a snooze. I wake up with John carrying me back to my room. I miaow in appreciation as he places me on my bed and places the blanket over me. Gemma makes her own way into her own bed, curls up, and falls asleep.

Chapter 12

Today

I WAKE UP HAVING HAD a dream about floating in a bath with model boats which are navigating around me on their own as I seem to float in the same place all the time. The boats seem to be working together to confuse me. There are submarines too, as I've seen their periscopes as they monitor me. All of a sudden, two crows arrive and start sinking the boats. They squawk at me… and then I wake up to see Gemma staring at me.

"You were twitching a lot, Frederick," says Gemma. "Are you bothered about something?"

"Yes, I was having a bath and there were lots of model boats ganging up on me, but then the crows arrived and sank some of them."

Gemma adopts her best psychiatrist pose, putting her head to one side and looking thoughtful and quizzical at the same time. She just needs a pair of glasses and a pen and paper, and the appearance would be complete.

"That's interesting, Frederick. This means that you're worried about going to the ship today and are expecting the crows to help you out at some point."

"Thank you. I was thinking the same thing, but there were a lot of ships around in my dream."

"Europoort is one of the biggest ports in the world, so there will be lots of ships around."

"Right, that makes sense. Thank you for your insight." I stretch my back legs and yawn before using the litter tray and having a snack from the fresh pile of kibbles that appeared magically as we were sleeping.

Gemma has found a book about first world war battles and is engrossed by its contents. In particular, she seems to enjoy the battles on the eastern front, such as Tannenberg and the Masurian Lakes, where there were two battles.

I decide to start reading *A Third Class Murder* and I like the book. It's a real page turner and the amateur detective is a clergyman who notices things the police seem to miss. This worries me slightly as I hope police outside in the real world are quicker to put things together than they are in the pages of this book. They don't seem thorough to me, and it makes me wonder how Gemma will portray the police in her book. Will they be a bunch of clodhoppers or will they be bright and smart? I am of half a mind to ask her, but she is reading her book of battles, and her tail is moving up and down with a rhythmic beat that suggests a certain amount of content. She is now reading about the battles in the Dolomites in northern Italy that were fought in terribly cold conditions between the Italians and the Austrians / Germans. I doubt there were any cats in those mountains, as they would be too sensible and stay at lower levels where it would be warmer and hopefully safer.

I trot outside to see who's around, and Mary and John are

both having a cup of coffee and a croissant each. John pours some water into a saucer and places that on a paving stone. I lap it up as it is a nice temperature, and I feel awake and alert afterwards.

Gemma comes out through the cat flap and squints in the morning sunshine. She has a good look around the garden and swipes her paw at two flies who come too close to her. I wonder if reading about battles is actually a good thing for her, as she seems agitated. Anyway, she soon comes over to where we are and sits down.

"Do you want some water, Gemma?" asks John.

Gemma looks at me: "Did you drink some water, is it straight out of the fridge?"

"I did. It's a nice temperature."

"I see," says Gemma and miaows at John, who puts the water in another saucer and places it carefully next to Gemma.

She laps up the water quickly and then looks up at John, who pours the remainder of the decanter into the saucer.

"They never drink so much water at home," says Mary, "they've adapted so quickly. I'll give them some croissant."

She tears a piece off her unfinished croissant and wafts it under my nose. I stare at her and not at the piece of pastry passing my proboscis, as I know taking a bite would not end well and I'll end up drooling wet pastry over my fur. Gemma eyes Mary as if to say, not for me either. Mary withdraws her hand.

John offers me part of a muffin and I reckon I'll enjoy better luck chewing this, as it has berries in it and quite a hard texture. I manage to keep most of the muffin in my mouth during the chewing, even placing my paw against my lips to make sure nothing slips out. It tastes lovely and so John feeds me some more.

"That's a bran muffin," says Gemma. "That should keep you regular, Frederick."

Gemma is a mine of useful information, and I marvel at her knowledge about bran muffins. It's not just battles with Gemma.

Miep appears along with Mrs Elkins, and they say hello to everyone and stroke both Gemma and myself. Miep has a fresh pot of coffee and both John and Mary drink a half cup each as they read their books.

Miep suggests they all go for a walk around the immediate area, so our human parents can get their bearings. I spy Henk in a tree, and I presume he'll use the opportunity to pass on the latest information to us.

Once the humans have gone for their extended walk, Henk swoops down and lands close to where Gemma and I are lying, enjoying the warmness and tranquillity.

"Good morning, English cats," says Henk, "I hope you enjoyed the humans' breakfast. It looked appetising."

"The muffin was good," I say. "I liked how chewy it was without disintegrating too much when I did chew it."

"Chewing, yes, that's something crows don't do, so I can't relate to what you're saying."

"That's probably a good thing, Henk," says Gemma, "as it means that you'll never visit the dentist and have your teeth checked and cleaned. I've been once, and it wasn't a pleasant experience. It involved anaesthetic, and I had a headache afterwards."

"I've been outside a dental practice observing someone's movements," replies Henk, "and there did seem to be a lot of unpleasant noises coming from the place, squealing drills and people gargling and trying to talk when their mouth is full of dental equipment."

I decide to keep quiet as I've never been to the dentist and so can add nothing to offer the conversation. From all I've heard, it doesn't sound like a nice experience.

"Anyway," says Henk, "we should talk a little about the business today. The ship has arrived on the tide and is being parked in the right place, as I'm speaking to you now. Miep and Mrs Elkins will accompany you down to Europoort in an unmarked police vehicle. You'll be introduced to the protestors near the Euromast. After about an hour, Miep will give you a ride down to the docks along with Bertie and Johann, who will be heading down to Euromast an hour after you. Are there any questions so far?"

Gemma shakes her head, as do I.

"You'll rendezvous with Cornelius, the big dachshund…"

"Rottweiler," says Gemma, "he's a Rottweiler."

"A German name, though," I say, "so similar, but a lot bigger."

"The Rottweiler, Cornelius, who will take you two and the squirrels to the ship, where you'll try to gain access to the ship. We're not sure if Cornelius will be able to accompany you around the ship, but he's been working on his athleticism, and he might surprise us as to where he gets to."

"Will you be there, Henk?" I ask.

"Yes, I'll be heading down there with the squirrels, me and two other crows will be going."

"That'll be a noisy journey," says Gemma. "Plenty of chatter."

"Yes, but we have a lot to prepare. Once you're on board, the crows will land on the ship and find where the crew are and then tell yourselves and the squirrels, so that Johann can distract them if necessary. Johann will be important for throwing the nuts at the crew."

"I get more nervous," says Gemma. "Every time we talk about it, I'll be fine once our work starts, but I suppose I'm impatient for us to begin."

"That's understandable," says Henk, "we've been after these people for months and this is the culmination of our efforts, so yes, I can understand that nervousness. What about you, Freddie?"

"I'm looking forward to the journey to the protest, attending the protest, and then let's see what happens after that. I'm trying not to look too far ahead."

"That's wise, Frederick," says Gemma. "Yes, the protest is important too, as we need to stop polluting the planet."

"Indeed, it is, and we'll have our photos taken again, so we'll be in the papers, but I wonder whether the people on the ship might not recognise us from those photos, even if they're under arrest and will know who we are."

"Yes, that's true," says Gemma, "and I worry they could find out where we live, if they don't know already."

"There's someone monitoring your house all the time,"

says Henk, "so don't worry too much about that. I know the crows watch your house and kick up a fuss whenever someone strange takes an interest in your house, even if it's a postman who's different from normal."

"That's good," says Gemma. "That's always been a concern of mine, because I don't want Mary and John to be harmed because of our activities."

"That's a relief to me too," I say.

"We do our best," says Henk. "I'm not sure we'll ask you to help us again for this reason. You are becoming well known and we can't risk you being seen and followed so that your safety and our operations become compromised as a result."

"I think that's wise," says Gemma. "As much as I like these trips, I think we have to evaluate how they affect our lives or could affect our lives."

"We should just concentrate on what happens today and talk about this afterwards," I say. "Let's see what happens today and what the consequences are, if any."

"That sounds sensible," says Gemma. "I agree."

"Living in the moment, that's good," says Henk, "I endorse that as a great way to live your life."

"Thank you," I reply. "I do my best to follow this way of thinking."

Two more crows, Arne, and Jan, then arrive and we are all introduced. Arne and Jan will be travelling with Henk and the two squirrels down to Europoort. Arne and Jan both have dark blue hues in their feathers, and I think I'll be able to recognise them should the need arise. A nut then hits me on the backside, announcing the arrival of Johann and

Bertie. I congratulate Johann on his accuracy as Bertie goes to retrieve the nut from where it has deflected under the table. No nut is ever wasted in Bertie's opinion. He puts the nut in his pouch.

"Freddie cat," says Johann, "I've seen recent videos of your friend Rufus, and he no longer lands on his face. This is a good thing for him."

Bertie giggles in agreement.

"Yes, I agree," I reply. "He's also trying to branch out into other areas, including swings. He wants to swing through the air."

"He's not heavy enough," says Bertie, "I understood those swings are made of thick wood and so even a cat would find it difficult to get them to move for even a few seconds. Plus, you have to land at the right angle to obtain the forward momentum."

"Yes, I've tried it, and I fell off," I say. "I don't think they were designed for cats or squirrels, just for the backsides of humans."

"Definitely," says Johann, "though it would be nice to try a smaller swing made from renewable plastic and see what it feels like."

Bertie giggles again, "How can we make that suggestion? We have some rope bridges in the trees, but a few small swings would be a good addition."

"I can type," says Gemma, "so if you know an email address, I can write down the suggestion and send it off. I think Mary has brought her travel computer with her, so I could use that."

"I have seen a notice on a nearby tree," says Bertie, "that contains an address. I'll just find it."

With that, Bertie leaps into a tree and disappears into the branches.

"Bertie has a lot of energy, all the time," says Johann. "I prefer to conserve mine for important occasions."

"He's brave," says Gemma, "I remember Bertie taunting Cornelius before the Rottweiler came over to our side and I was impressed at Bertie's quick reactions, although Cornelius did telegraph his intentions."

There is a cawing in the trees from two crows.

"The humans are returning," says Arne, "they're about three hundred yards away."

Gemma looks at me and seems to be impressed. Arne appears excellent at deciphering caws, which to me all sounded the same.

Henk notices the feline exchange of looks: "Our crows are very good at providing information, and the ones down at Europoort are the best we have."

"And the loudest," adds Jan. "There can be a lot of noise and so they have to make themselves heard above all that."

"I see," says Gemma, "but I suppose the humans don't take any notice, as they're concentrating on their work."

"Yes, the ones who are up to no good are looking out for humans wearing uniforms rather than working clothes and ignore the birds," says Arne, "This is good from our point of view, of course."

We soon hear the voices of the humans as they talk about what they'd just seen.

"Right, Gemma and Freddie," says Henk, "we should go and leave you here. You'll be leaving soon, and we'll see you down at Europoort later, in about four hours' time. Have a good journey down there, although you'll be in a police vehicle, so no one will come close to you. Enjoy your protest and don't be surprised if you receive a lot of attention. The English cats are well known, which is going to make it difficult for you to leave the protest, but we have a good idea, we think, but I won't say any more about that. See you later."

The crows flap away and Johann waves at us before heading up the trunk of the nearest tree. Bertie suddenly appears and provides Gemma with an email address he's found on a park sign. Knowing Gemma, she won't forget the email.

The humans come through the gate to find Gemma and me on the grass, contemplating our existence in the sunshine.

"Here they are," says Mary, "having a rest before their trip down to the protest. How clever they are."

"Cats tend to have a rest most of the time," says Mrs Elkins, "before a sudden burst of activity."

"I'm sure they're in good hands," says John as he gave us both a stroke, "and they're not going to be away for too long."

"Just a few hours," says Miep, looking quizzically at Gemma, who is managing to tolerate John's attention without showing too much displeasure.

Miep looks at Mrs Elkins and then says: "Gemma and Freddie, we should be leaving in ten minutes, as you can never be sure about the traffic, and we do need to be there in plenty of time."

I do a self-evaluation and decide I need to have a poo

before leaving, so I scoot back to our room and do the necessary. I'm unsure whether we will be in our carriers or not, so I decide to grab my book and carry that in my mouth outside.

"That's a good idea," says Gemma, "but my book is a bit too heavy for me to carry."

Gemma miaows and then rubs herself around Mrs Elkins's legs before trotting off towards the door. Mrs Elkins smiles and follows Gemma, returning a few moments later with the book in her hand, closely followed by Gemma.

"Well," says Miep, "we may as well go as the cats seem to be ready. I'm not sure what the leaders of the protest are expecting of the cats, but they'll probably be photographed with a placard about environmental pollution. Would that be alright, Mary and John?"

"I'm sure that will be fine," says Mary. "I'm not sure whether oil companies can sue animals for any reason…?"

"No, they can't, nor their owners, especially if the owners are not present. But all that's going to happen is that Gemma and Freddie will have their picture taken a lot with many other people. The cats will be showing international solidarity with their friends in the Netherlands as people were really fascinated by their performances at the various events they've attended in the past few weeks."

With that Mrs Elkins picks up our books and Mary and John give us a stroke and tell us they look forward to seeing us later at the Rijksmuseum. We miaow and then follow Miep across the lawn as she heads towards her garden gate. Another little adventure is about to begin.

==========

Gemma and I trot after Miep and Mrs Elkins as we head towards the closest road. There is a large, dark-blue vehicle with three rows of seats. The front two seats are already occupied by two men with short haircuts who get out of the van as the two ladies arrive. They salute and open the doors for us.

"So, these are the cats?" asks one of them.

"They are," says Miep, "Freddie and Gemma, please meet Robbie and Marco, who'll be driving us today."

We miaow and Gemma offers the two men her right paw by way of welcome. The two men shake Gemma's paw and scratch me under my chin.

"Gemma and Freddie, we're going to put a collar on each of you now. This will contain a tracking device, so we know where you are at all times," says Mrs Elkins.

Once this operation is complete, we jump into the back row of the vehicle and find that there are two children's carriers, one for each of us. Both are dark blue and stand out against the cream-coloured interior. There is a seatbelt too and Miep straps us in so that we can read our book or stare out of the window. There is a smell of freshly cleaned upholstery. We both have a water bottle, similar to a human baby's bottle, where we can suck a teat and obtain water in just the correct amount. This is a great idea. Gemma enjoys it because it gives her more independence.

Robbie drives us away, gently at first, because there are many cyclists around who are enjoying the weather and warm temperatures. We don't want to draw attention to ourselves too much as we head out of the city towards Rotterdam. Gemma isn't looking out of the window too much, but is concentrating on her book of battles on the Western front in World War I. The names of some of them read like a bad set of tiles to have in your hand when playing Scrabble, which Mary and John sometimes do.

I read some of my book and enjoy it very much, although the village police seem to have missed some rather obvious questions. When I think it through, if the police did get everything right, then the amateur detective wouldn't have much of a role in the book and could have stayed at home composing sermons for his flock of churchgoers. This might not have made a very interesting book to read. The clergyman also has a dog that is useful, as it finds sacks of discarded clothes lying by the railway line. This shows that dogs do have their uses, even in fictional literature. I should mention this to Gemma, as no dogs are scheduled to appear in her pet shop detectives' book. Perhaps a dog could find a vital clue? Or put the kettle on when the pet detectives return?

Rivers are important around Rotterdam, so I will provide a few names for you. After entering the Netherlands, the Rhine splits into numerous branches. The main branch is called the Waal, which flows from Nijmegen to meet the Meuse thereafter called Merwede. Near Rotterdam, the river is known as Nieuwe Maas and becomes the Nieuwe Waterweg flowing into the North Sea at Hook of Holland. This is where the ferries from Harwich in England arrive. The Oude Maas, or Old Meuse, is a distributary of the river Rhine, and a former distributary of the river Maas. A distributary is a river that flows out of a river rather than into another river, which is what a tributary does. The Old Meuse begins at the city of Dordrecht, where the Beneden Merwede river splits into the Noord and the Oude Maas. It ends when it joins the Nieuwe Maas to form Het Scheur. I hope you're keeping up with all these names. They're all rivers and the ships don't really mind what the name of the water is they're floating on.

After about ninety minutes, we arrive on the outskirts of Rotterdam, and I can see the Euromast near where the protest will take place. Gemma is still reading her book, and I have almost finished mine. I think I know who's done it, but I decide to keep the revelation until later and to observe the world passing by.

Miep turns around to speak to me and Gemma.

"Gemma and Freddie, we're about five minutes away. You'll be meeting a lady called Rosita, who is originally from the country of Colombia, but now lives here for half the year. There will be many people there, but after an hour, we'll leave quietly once the photos and interviews have taken place."

Gemma looks at me and says: "This is where it begins, Frederick." She then starts reading her book again, but I am too excited to read and peer round with curiosity.

We soon pull over to the side of the road where numerous people are waiting for something. Most of them are carrying placards and smiling. I can see the slender Euromast with its bulging observation deck at its halfway point nearby.

Miep opens her door and gets out, shaking hands with a smaller lady with greying hair and a lovely smile. Gemma stops her reading.

"That must be Rosita. She looks very distinguished. What do you think? With that stylish grey hair and those large glasses?"

"She looks nice. I see there's someone with a camera, so we're going to be on film again."

"Well, at least Mary and John know we're here. That's what worries me, when we're sort of going behind their backs and taking part in events they're not aware of."

"I know what you mean. We should try to enjoy this part before the hard work begins."

Mrs Elkins opens the door closest to me and I jump down from the carrier onto the mat, put there for human feet, and then out of the door onto the concrete of the pavement. Gemma follows me down and we both stand looking up at the mass of strangers towering over us. All of them seem happy. Some are wearing bobble hats and waterproof jackets, while others hold umbrellas in one hand and a placard in the other. The cause of the protest seems to be related to the pollution of the water by discharged oil.

Miep comes over to us and crouches down so we can listen to her.

"Gemma and Freddie, Mrs Elkins and I will wait here for you. You'll be back in an hour or so and we'll drive a short distance and then I'll cycle you to the rendezvous point with the others. By then, the squirrels and the crows will be here, we'll walk to meet Cornelius. No humans will be with you from then on. Cornelius will walk you to the ship and then you will go on board and find the human prisoners. Once you find them, let Cornelius know and he'll bark three times. That will be the signal for us to arrive and make sure the crew don't escape. Johann will distract the crew if necessary, and Bertie will untie them if they are bound up. The crows will be all over the ship and will help if help is required. Anyway, here's Rosita and her friend Rosemary, who will take care of you. They may pick you up to show you off to the cameras as the English cats who've come over to the Netherlands to support a worthy cause. See you later." She rubs both our heads in her gentle manner before turning around and introducing us to Rosita and Rosemary.

Rosita kneels down and admires us: "The famous English protest cats, who will help us get our message across to the authorities and to people across Europe." She clasps her hands together and then strokes Gemma, who's been looking at her with something approaching enthusiasm. Gemma purrs a little.

"That cat likes you," says the lady called Rosemary. "You should carry that one and I'll take this one, who's been looking at me a bit apprehensively."

I wasn't aware of looking apprehensive or even worried, but I miaow as she lifts me up and cuddles me.

"This one is a well-fed cat," says Rosemary. "He weighs a lot."

Gemma looks across at me with a slight smirk.

"This one too," says Rosita.

Gemma's smirk transforms into a slight glare in an instant. I sniff the breeze and think how lucky we both are to have such good human parents who feed us on a regular basis.

"This one is called Freddie, right?" says Rosemary.

"He's the male cat, yes, Freddie, and this one I have is the female cat, Gemma," replies Rosita.

We are walking along at the head of the march towards the Euromast and approaching us are a number of film crews, along with interviewers holding microphones that appear like fluffy ice cream cones.

We soon stop. The cameras are pointed at us as people wave their placards around behind us.

At the base of The Euromast, we stop again, and the interviewers ask Rosita and Rosemary questions and then ask both Gemma and myself in English how we like the Netherlands. We both miaow enthusiastically and wave a paw at the camera. More people arrive as we start walking along the paths towards what appears to be a park. There are various pathways through the green space, with people having picnics on the grass and others reading whilst trying to get tanned. I think the idea is to get people to join us on our walk through the park. We arrive at a fountain depicting three dancers and circle around this feature before heading back to the Euromast, where more people are waiting. On a patch of open ground, a small stage has been set up. Gemma and I are introduced to the crowd of about three hundred people. Many photographers take our pictures, and I hope that this will help the protesters get their message across. Gemma seems to like having her picture taken and doesn't glare at anyone. Eventually, Rosita and Rosemary sit down on a couple of plastic chairs and we both jump down to sit together where more pictures are taken of the English cats enjoying the Rotterdam sunshine. Someone produces a small placard and places it in front of us. Many pictures are taken of this photogenic scene. Rosemary and Rosita both give us a hug before we trot off the stage and sit down in the grass at the side. The important speeches are about to start, and no one wants there to be any feline distractions. There is some chanting, and a song is sung before a local green activist starts to speak using a microphone. The atmosphere feels incredibly positive, and I am so pleased to be part of the experience.

Then, out of the corner of my eye, I spy a familiar crow figure. Henk gives a squawk and waves a wing at me. This seems like a signal. We follow him out under the stage as he hops like a corvine wallaby to the edge of the path. No one seems to know we've left. We scurry along the path until we see our vehicle up ahead, with Miep and Mrs Elkins resting against its side.

"Hello, kitties," says Miep, "you're already popular on social media, especially when you have that placard in front of you. 'Make our water clean' is what it says. Now you should get inside quickly, before anyone takes a picture of us all together."

We miaow, the writing on the placard is a good message to get across to people, most of whom take their waterways for granted, no matter what those waterways are called. We jump inside and decide to lie low rather than stare out of the window. Cats normally operate by stealth, and this is an appropriate time to put this into practice. We seem to go through a security gate and then come to a stop in the shadow of what turned out to be a warehouse.

The doors open, and we slink out of the vehicle. We both lie low and peer at the docks, at the containers, cranes, oil drums, and lorries. There isn't too much human activity going on, but there is a lot of evidence that there will be in the near future. Cranes are loading containers on one ship and from another. A second vehicle arrives and out hops Bertie and Johann, plus Arne and Jan. Henk has already landed and now a bicycle miraculously appears with a large basket on the back.

"Okay, kitties and squirrels, your taxi awaits," says Miep, gesturing towards the bicycle.

The squirrels leap into the basket whereas Gemma and I allow ourselves to be loaded into it, thanks to Mrs Elkins. The three crows perch on the side and Miep speeds away towards the berth of our ship.

"Have you been here before?" asks Gemma to Johann and Bertie.

"No," says Bertie, "it's a long way to come for a squirrel under normal circumstances. The furthest I've ever been is about three miles from Vondelpark, and that was when I got lost one day."

"I'm the same," says Johann. "I'm not sure I could live somewhere like this, as there are too many buildings and not enough green space."

"Yes, everything is very stark, isn't it?" I say. "Very man-made and unnatural and artificial."

"Yes, you'd think they'd have a few gardens and flowers around, just to give people something to smile about," says Gemma, "just to provide a bit of variety in the landscape."

In the distance, I locate a black speck that I sort of recognise. It has a pair of ears, a very muscular frame, and is sitting in the shadows.

Miep pedals towards the speck and we all see that it is indeed our friend Cornelius who seems even larger than I remember him. All that exercise has made him a large dog, and I am glad he is on our side. Miep cycles into the shadows and stops. The crows flap off as if they know exactly where they are going. The squirrels leap out of the basket. Miep lifts up Gemma and me and places us on the ground. We miaow our thanks and scamper off towards Cornelius, who is standing up and wagging his tail furiously.

Cornelius walks towards us and then he whispers: "Hello, it's good to work with you all. The ship we are interested in is about four hundred yards behind me on your right. We shouldn't make any unnecessary noise. Please follow me in line and I'll stop when we get to the bottom of the gangplank. You can then gain access to the ship and find out where the people are. There are definitely trafficked people on board because I've heard them moaning towards the stern of the ship, but it's down to you to find them, Gemma and Freddie. I've identified a place for Johann to watch out for crew members to distract and throw nuts at."

"That's great," I whisper. "How many crew have you seen?"

"I've seen five on board walking on deck and they were armed with large sticks and possibly revolvers, but I can't say that for sure. Anyway, we should head down there and start this operation. When you find the people, Gemma and

Freddie, come and tell me and I'll bark. Then our human friends will arrive."

Gemma looks at me with determination and smiles. She is back in spy mode and in her element. She walks after Cornelius, and I follow her. Johann and Bertie hitch a ride on Cornelius, as that's what squirrels do.

We scamper down to the ship, which looms over the dock. I can see the gangplank coming down to the dockside and then, all of a sudden, it strikes me that we are doing something dangerous. My mouth is dry, and I wish I was under the couch at home reading a book. But I don't want to let anyone down, as people are relying on me, including the people who are being kept illegally on the ship. There is only one way off the ship and once we are on board, it will be easy to trap us. I peer along the side of the ship and there is nowhere to leap from that isn't at least ten feet off the ground. The rails are round and not easy to balance on. The red paint is flaking in places, exposing bare metal, rusty in places.

Cornelius comes to a halt, and we stop in the shadows.

"Good luck," Cornelius says. "Remember, I think the noises I heard were coming from the back of the ship."

"Right," says Gemma, "let's get to the top of the gangplank and find out where we should go from there. I'd guess the people will be held in a hold under the main deck, so we ought to find a way to go down."

With that, she scoots to the bottom of the gangplank and hides. She looks upwards to check that no one is watching and then scurries to the top, with me close behind. Gemma is very decisive when she doesn't know where she's going, but she says that it's better to do it this way as you have to find out where you stand as soon as possible. We have a scout around and see a squirrel above us on top of a mast, possibly a radio mast. There's an open doorway ahead of us and we peer inside. It appears to be someone's cabin with lots of clothing on the floor and a tap dripping in the washbasin. A toothpaste top is on the floor.

Suddenly a voice says "Well, well, I didn't know we had cats on this ship. That would explain why there are no rats." We turn around, sit down, and miaow at the rather burly bearded man holding a phone who almost blocks the doorway. He approaches us and then clutches the back of his neck before looking around. We take our chance and scamper past him, one on either side, in a move designed to disorient the human.

We run along the deck and hide. We owe our first debt of gratitude to Johann the squirrel. The man comes out of the door and heads away from us. After about ten seconds, he talks to someone and his sentence definitely contains the word 'cat', so I presume he is checking to discover whether this vessel does have official ship's cats.

"Freddie," says Gemma, "there's a doorway over there and some steps heading downwards. Let's take a peek."

She zooms over there, and I am left in her wake. Gemma is heading down the steps when I make an observation.

"This could well be the way down to the engine room, as the air is stiflingly hot."

"It could well be. I'll scoot down and check."

With that, she disappears downwards, and I wait patiently but alertly by the door, making sure I am out of sight.

Gemma is gone for about five minutes, and I begin to worry. A dripping sound comes from underneath where I am sitting, and I peer over the edge of the metal floor. There is a view of the engine room with metal flooring running between the machinery. The flooring is on two levels below where I am. Gemma is trotting along, looking at the large metal items as though she is on a tour of the engine room. There is no space down there for any holds and so I can't understand why we should hang around any longer, as no people are being smuggled down there. I hiss at her, but I don't think she hears me, so I scoot down the steps and scurry along to where I'd last seen her.

"Gemma," I say, "where are you?"

"I'm here," she replies. "I'm admiring the size of these engines, and this isn't even a big ship in tonnage terms." She is standing above me on what appears to be a large metal pipe.

"We should be going," I say. "The people aren't going to be down here."

"Well, there might be some," replies Gemma, scowling slightly. "There's another door at the end of this gangway, so let's find out what's through there. I looked and there are two further doorways, so let's have a look. There might be people in there."

She jumps down beside me, and we head along to the doorway she's told me about. We hop over the threshold where there are two further doorways, both with windows. There seems to be a slight rim at the edge of the glass on one of the windows, and I think I might be able to grip this rim with my claws. I tell Gemma my idea and she agrees it is worth a try. I stand at the foot of the door and jump up vertically but miss and slide down the metal door. I adjust my back paws slightly and jump again. This time, one of my claws sticks in the rim and I am able to use my other claws to hold myself in place. The only thing is, it appears my claw has caught in the rim and is well and truly stuck. Anyway, first things first. I pull myself up to try to get my nose to the window. This is more difficult than pulling myself up the trellis.

"There are human footsteps," says Gemma. I watch as she looks out into the engine room.

"There's three of them, and they're each carrying something. They're two floors up, but they seem to be heading down the steps."

I tell myself that I can do this, that I can really do this, and I haul my nose up to the glass.

"They're coming down the steps."

I raise myself another three inches and I can see into the space behind the glass. There are people inside lying down, though they are shadowy forms, as the only light is coming from the engine room.

"There are people in there, at least a few people."

"They're coming down the second set of steps. You should detach yourself."

"I can't, my claw's stuck. Can you jump up underneath me and give me a nudge upwards to give impetus to my front right leg and I can dislodge my claw?"

"Can't you retract it?" asks Gemma.

"I've tried. It won't retract."

Gemma sits underneath me and jumps upwards. It does no good.

"Do that again, but on the count of three."

"Okay."

"One, two, three..."

Gemma launches herself into my right side and as she does so, I move my right front leg forwards using her impetus and dislodge my claw. We fall in a heap on the floor. "Quick, outside on our right," says Gemma.

We scamper over the threshold and hide behind a vertical pipe. I try to calm my heart pounding in my chest by closing my eyes and thinking of my mum.

The three men soon appear around the corner, and we note they are carrying trays with plastic water bottles on them, plus what appear to be slices of bread. They all step over the threshold. Using our natural stealth, Gemma and I slide across the side of the threshold and peer over it. One of the men puts his tray on the ground and takes a large set of keys from his belt. He unlocks the nearer door and pushes the tray into the room beyond. Before the door is closed and locked, two or three hands reach for the items on the tray. The man unlocks the other door, and the other two trays are placed on the floor.

"We should go, we've found the people," says Gemma. "Let's get out before they find us. Let's get to Cornelius."

We scamper off and run up the metal steps, past the thrumming engines, with our eyes fixed on the door to the outside world.

Halfway up the last set of steps, I hear one of the men behind us shout out some words that almost certainly contain the word cat and I am relieved when we arrive back on deck and are able to breathe in fresh air and experience some cooler temperatures. My paws are damp from sweat and I have blood under one of my claws.

"There's people coming, let's go this way," says Gemma and we head to the seaward side of the ship.

"Let's hide and discuss what we're doing. This way is away from Cornelius."

We stop in a doorway.

"We should split," I say, "one of us should lead them on a wild goose chase and the other should head to the gangplank and tell Cornelius to start barking."

"Great idea," says Gemma. "I'll lead them away from the gangplank and you then head to the gangplank."

"Hello," says three voices. We glance up and see Bertie, Johann, and Henk.

"Have you found them?" asks Henk.

"Yes," says Gemma, "Freddie is going to tell Cornelius, and I'm going to lead the crew away from the gangplank."

"Wait a second," says Henk, "I'll check where the crew are."

"Me too," says Bertie, "they're moving around a lot at the moment."

Henk flies off and Bertie runs up a nearby duct. Johann climbs on to a cabin roof to check the immediate surroundings. He carries a nut in his paw just in case he needs it.

"Right, they're all on the land side of the ship," says

Bertie, returning in his usual nonchalant manner, "I have an idea how you can get to Cornelius, but I'll wait for Henk. The way to the gangplank from here is left, right, down the steps, left, down the steps, and right."

I close my eyes and memorise the route… it sounds nearby.

Henk returns and has a discussion with Johann and Bertie.

"Right," says Henk, "I think we have a plan. At the end of this passage, there are two directions, left towards the land and right towards the sea. Johann will go and throw nuts at the men down below from the end of the left-hand passage and then wave at them to bring them up here. When they come up here, Gemma should sit at the end of the right-hand passage, clearly visible. Bertie will also sit with her but show his tail to make them think he is really the Freddie cat. The crows will then caw loudly above Gemma to draw their attention. When they start to run towards Gemma, Gemma runs away. Bertie climbs on to the roof, and Freddie heads to the left. Arne and Jan will fly above Freddie and distract anyone who approaches him. I'll stick with Gemma and will provide any help I can, though I'm sure she won't need it. There is a man on the gangplank, but we'll attack him along with three other dock crows, so Freddie can get to Cornelius. He'll bark and then the humans will arrive."

We nod our agreement, and Johann heads off to start the distractions. Gemma winks at me and she and Bertie trot off to sit at the right-hand end of the passageway. Presently, there is some shouting, and Johann indicates the people are coming our way.

"Good luck, Freddie cat," says Henk and flies off to start the racket that will attract the men to Gemma's position. Arne and Jan arrive. I recognise the colour palette of their feathers, and they motion for me to stay still for a moment. Five men appear and the other crows near Gemma start their racket. Some pointing takes place, and the men run towards Gemma. Arne takes off and swoops up and down before calling out, "You're free to go, Freddie."

I scoot away and follow Bertie's instructions with Arne and Jan in close attendance. Ahead, a man is standing facing away from me, but I bolt past him. He shouts and then starts swatting at the crows, seeming to catch Jan on the wing, and he falls to the deck. Jan struggles up and hops away. I am near the gangplank now, but two men are running towards me and in my path. I stop and sit. Arne flies ahead, then comes up behind the man nearer the cabins, and pecks him on the head. The man puts this hand up to protect himself and I zoom past him, hugging the metal walls of the cabins. The other man couldn't stop me, as his fellow crew member was in the way.

There is a man on the gangplank, but suddenly his world changes as he has a lot of problems to deal with, namely four crows doing their impressions of angry hornets buzzing around his head. I sneak past and call out to Cornelius to start his barking.

Cornelius barks. I tell Arne to check that Jan is okay as he seems to have a damaged wing, and Arne flies off to find him. Three cars draw up within a minute. I wait to see Miep and then miaow at her.

"Freddie, you've found them. Show us." I scoot up the

gangplank followed by some large police officers and then head to the engine room, making sure I don't get too far ahead, because as you know, cats can run faster than humans when motivated. Down the stairs I go and arrive at the doorway. I sit down and look around. Miep arrives and says: "They're in here?" I miaow.

Miep turns and speaks to the people behind her. I think the crew are being rounded up, given the amount of shouting I heard as I ran along the deck, so hopefully the police find the man who has the keys to these doors. I presume Miep is making it clear we have to find the keys, as most of them disappear up the stairs.

"You've hurt your paw, Freddie," says Miep, "let me have a look. I'll try not to hurt you."

I hold up my paw and Miep takes it gently. She takes a bottle of water from her jacket and pours some of it over my paw. She takes out a tube of antibiotics from another pocket and rubs some of it on the claw. It stings a little, but it feels as though it is doing me good, though it is also the power of having positive thoughts that does me good, almost as though I'm using ESP on myself. I hear shouting and see a member of the crew being frogmarched down the stairs by a pair of large men who are practically carrying him along. The clanging of their boots reverberates around the engine room. Thankfully, I see Gemma scurrying along behind, followed by Cornelius and the two squirrels who again hitch a lift on the large dog, who doesn't seem to notice their presence on his back.

The crew member, clutching the keys, is plonked

unceremoniously over the threshold and rather reluctantly places the key in the lock of the first door. The door is opened, and nothing happens for a few seconds. One of the policemen looks inside and then steps into the room, beckoning to Miep to follow. Miep quickly radios and gestures for the other door to be opened.

Altogether, thirty-five people are in those two small holds. Some have their hands tied and Bertie is able to free them. Bertie has small paws, but he's got strong front legs, and the cord holds no problems for him. The people shuffle out of their confinement and some trip over the threshold before being helped up the stairs.

Gemma looks at the people with hooded eyebrows and is obviously upset by their state. I close my eyes and try to meditate for a minute, to calm myself, and perhaps try to start to reconcile what motivates people to be so obnoxious to their fellow human beings. When I open my eyes, Gemma still seems discombobulated. She walks into the room and looks around, wrinkling her nose, as some people had obviously been seasick recently.

I try to take her mind off them: "How are you, Gemma? Did your pursuers get close to you?"

"No, I jumped up onto a roof and they couldn't get to me. They brought a step ladder, so I jumped onto another roof, and they got upset. Then they heard cars drawing up and self-preservation took over, and they tried to scarper, but of course there's only one way off the ship, and so they were hooped. How could those nasty humans imprison their fellows? Other species don't do that. Humans are so self-destructive."

"Did any of your pursuers jump overboard?"

"One did, but a patrol boat caught him before he could swim very far. I hope the prisoners are alright, it must have been so traumatic to be cooped up in there for days with so little room."

"How are you, Cornelius?" I ask.

"I'm very well," says Cornelius, "you seemed to find the people very quickly."

"That's my fault," says Gemma, "I'm really interested in machinery and how things work, and I was distracted by the size of the engines. We saw the doorway here and we investigated, and Freddie went all athletic and hauled himself up to look through the window."

"How did you do that?" Johann asks me.

I explain how I manage to catch a claw on the rim of the window and then pull myself up.

Bertie grips my front leg and says: "This English cat has strong front legs from climbing up the trellis at his house. I have seen the videos on the internet."

I smile, but I am absolutely stunned. I had no idea pictures of me were on the internet, climbing into my own house. Part of me feels violated. Who has done this? I think I will tell the Lancashire rose she is on the internet the next time I see her, though she may not fully comprehend what this means.

Gemma looks surprised too, but our conversation is interrupted by the return of Miep, who says we can now leave the engine room as all the crew and the prisoners are safely on the dockside. She checks my paw again and seems satisfied it is alright.

We head out into the daylight. Most of the sky is a light grey colour, but some rays of sunshine are bravely making their way through, creating some yellow pockets of brightness. I look around and realise how much we all take for granted on a daily basis. Even spending thirty minutes inside the ship made me appreciate the faint sunlight glinting off the metal of the cabins and superstructure. There is a light breeze, and I enjoy the feeling that Mother Nature is welcoming me back by ruffling my fur slightly as we head off the ship and back on to dry land.

We say au revoir to Cornelius, who will now enjoy a few days off from patrolling at Europoort. Henk, Arne, and Jan arrive. Jan has to hop as his wing is damaged, although, according to the resident vet on the docks, he should be fine after resting for a few days. We all share a large SUV on our quiet journey back to Amsterdam as we all take time to reflect on what has just happened in our own ways. My claw seems to be healing nicely, thanks to Miep. My heart is still racing, though I am content to be safe. Gemma has curled up and fallen asleep, although she does twitch sometimes, indicating she is still jumping around the superstructure of the ship in her dreams. Gemma adapts so quickly to new situations that I can't help wondering whether she shouldn't be a full-time spy cat, serving king and country for the good of all. Bertie and Johann have taken off their rucksacks and are resting on them in a lethargic manner with their front paws clasped. The crows sit in their paper box and close their eyes.

We arrive back at Miep's house where the police vet picks up Jan and takes him to the animal hospital so he can have his wing set. He also looks at my claw and says I should keep it clean and then it will heal quickly, as I am obviously a healthy cat. Henk and Arne say they'll see us outside The Rijksmuseum later on and fly off, presumably to have some food. The squirrels are asleep, so Miep and Mrs Elkins put them on the garden table to let them wake up naturally rather than jolting them awake. Gemma and I launch ourselves at the cat flap and eat some kibbles and use the litter tray. We are soon back out in the garden where Mrs Elkins is enjoying a cup of tea.

"Gemma and Freddie," she says, putting her cup down on the saucer, "I know you can understand me. You rescued thirty-five people today. There were thirty-five people in those holds you found next to the engine room, so as to disguise any shouting those people might have made to try to attract attention. It was very clever of you to work that out."

Gemma looks at me: "It was only because I was interested in machinery that you found them. It's strange how life works sometimes, isn't it?"

"Yes, it is," I reply before miaowing at Mrs Elkins. Gemma looks at Mrs Elkins and nods her head ever so slightly.

Miep comes out looking a little glamorous in a skirt and wearing dangling earrings. It would appear it is time to go to the reception at the Rijksmuseum. She looks at my paw and seems impressed at my immune system, which is doing a good job of healing my claw. We trot after Miep as she heads to her bicycle. We jump in the basket and the memories come flooding back of our time only a few short weeks ago. Things haven't changed much along the canals since our last visit as we head towards the Rijksmuseum, where previously we'd had our own personal tour on a tea trolley.

Miep shows her security pass to the police guard and places her bike in a rack. We jump down and look around at the people who are milling about in front of the entrance, some of whom are more anxious to be seen than others.

"Miep's probably in charge of the security for the event," says Gemma, "so let's hope nothing untoward occurs."

"I hope no one tries to steal a painting this time," I say. "That can't happen."

Miep beckons to us and we head through a side entrance where no people are trampling around without looking where they are putting their feet.

"Mary and John are on the second floor," says Miep, pointing up the stairs, "having a private tour, but not on a tea trolley like you." I miaow aloud and Gemma puts her paw on my mouth after five seconds to show that I've gone on too long. She is probably right, she usually is.

We walk along the corridor towards the growing noise of human voices in a large room. Miep heads up to a balcony where we all have a view of the people who are admiring paintings and having drinks and small snacks served to them. Gemma and I jump onto the bannister to look at the people.

"Gemma and Freddie," says Miep, "do you recognise anyone?"

Gemma looks at me: "Who needs closed-circuit television and artificial intelligence when there are cats to scan the crowd?"

"Indeed, I wonder why she's asking. I thought everyone we saw had been arrested."

"Perhaps from the house you went inside?"

"Yes, could be, I'll look around," I reply. I stare at the people who are enjoying the hospitality and don't recognise anyone, probably because most of them are in their 'glad rags' as John would say or 'posh frocks' as Mary would say. 'Formal attire' is what most people would understand these expressions to mean. All of a sudden, my fur feels as though it is standing on end. There is someone there I recognise, someone I've seen in the house that Gemma mentioned, the person who brought in the dog whose bowl I had eaten from. This person is serving small sandwiches from a large tray. I stare at Miep and then back at the sandwich server.

"Freddie, what have you seen?" asks Miep.

I point out the man to Gemma, who describes him back as wearing a black bow tie, white suit, formal shirt, and dark-grey trousers, to confirm she has the correct person. Gemma has slipped into spy mode again.

"Who are you watching, Freddie? The man with the sandwiches on the tray?" asks Miep.

We both miaowed. Yes, that was him.

"He nodded at the server over there walking around with the glasses of what I presume is sparkling wine," says Gemma. "I'm watching the drinks person in case he leaves. Do you recognise the drinks person?"

"No, I don't, but he has few drinks left and so he might go and replenish his supply any moment." The man gives two more drinks away.

"He's just drunk the last glass himself," says Gemma. "That's suspicious. I'm going to follow him."

She jumps down onto the ground and looks at Miep.

"It's okay, Gemma and Freddie. We can track you using your collars, so you can follow people if you wish."

Gemma miaows and heads down the stairs to follow the man, who is walking away with his tray under his arm. I am now suspicious, as this appears to be a diversion of some kind. It also strikes me that Miep is expecting us to recognise someone, almost as though the security services had a tip-off, and they need some stealthy operators on hand in case there is substance to the rumour. I look at the sandwich server as he glances at his watch. He expects something to happen, and I reckon I should be closer to him when it happens. I miaow at Miep, and she nods to me, showing me her phone displaying two dots on a map. One is moving, presumably Gemma, so I should start moving too. I look at the screen, make eye contact with Miep, and miaow to show I understand. I find the server and make a beeline for him, well actually a 'catline' with lots of twists and turns in it to avoid the humans and their careless feet. The man is walking through the crowd having put his food platter down on a spare table. He stops and looks through a window. Almost imperceptibly, he nods his head. An alarm sounds from the other side of the ground floor galleries. My guess is that this is the diversion that Gemma is investigating and probably involves an attempt to steal a painting or some other item from the collection. The question is: what is the sandwich server going to do, if the alarm is the diversion? I am near the entrance. Most people are making their way towards the sound of the alarm and are distracted.

Suddenly, the man grabs a young woman wearing a red dress who is sitting on a chair, puts handcuffs on her, and carries her off with him. He is strong. I zoom after him as he heads outside. On the side of the museum, a window has been broken, and a man is running away, causing the security people to follow him. The sandwich server passes the girl over the security barrier to another man. Now there's a problem. I see two crows, one of whom I recognise.

"Arne," I say, "I'll follow the girl, you follow the man."

"Okay, Freddie," says Arne, "take care of yourself. Famke here will follow you, so you will be supported."

"Good," I say, "hello, Famke."

Famke waves in the same friendly way as all the other crows in the Netherlands and we watch the man carry the girl towards a larger Sports Utility Vehicle or SUV as they're called by humans who like initialisms. Someone inside opens the back door, and the kidnapped lady is unceremoniously dumped on the backseat. The door closes. The man who carried the lady gets into the front beside the driver. There is a spare tyre on the back of the black vehicle, and I jump onto that, finding a cat-sized crevice to hide in as the vehicle speeds off in as unobtrusive a way as possible. Famke has found a spot to perch on too, on the broad spokes of the wheel.

"This is good, Freddie cat," she says, "we shouldn't be seen by the people in the vehicle until they stop and get out."

"Yes," I say, "can you hold on alright, Famke?"

"I can brace my legs, so I should be okay until we stop, and then I might fall off, but I can spread my wings, so I'll be okay. How about you?"

"Yes, I should be fine. Thank you for asking. I wonder where we're going?"

"Well, by the looks of it, eastwards towards Ijsselmeer so far, but that can soon change."

"Do you know who the girl is?" I ask.

"No, I don't, it seems as though it was planned though. We had no reports of anyone planning anything. The higher-ups might have heard some rumours, but they didn't tell us. Your visit might not have been entirely coincidental. We were on duty like we normally are on occasions like this."

"Henk and Arne were down at Europoort with us this afternoon," I say, "so I'd expect them to have a rest and not be on duty."

"Well, they were hoping to perch in a tree for four hours too and rest, but trouble seems to follow you around or perhaps it's the other way around?"

I laugh and think that trouble seems to find Gemma and I whenever we leave home. The vehicle takes a right turn and seems to be heading out of the city.

"They are following us," says Famke, "there's a police vehicle, unmarked of course, about one hundred metres behind. It's turning now. I recognise the number plate. There's a crow on the sign facing our way and it cawed twice. There's a locator on your collar and they'll follow that until this vehicle stops."

Some bemused people in the car behind are looking at us

through their windscreen. I don't suppose you often see a cat and a crow hitching a ride on a tyre on the back of a vehicle. I start to worry that they'll pull alongside the driver and tell them about their passengers, but then I realise that the driver of our vehicle wouldn't want anyone looking into his SUV and would ignore them. If I'd kidnapped someone, I wouldn't want anyone looking into my getaway car, that's for sure. Call me protective if you like.

We continue to drive, and Famke tells me we are still heading eastwards, so we're moving away from the airport and Europoort. I wonder if we're driving to a private house or country estate where the victim will be held, and a ransom note delivered?

The sun is setting, and vehicles have their lights on. The skeletal shapes of trees appear in profile against the reddening sky, adding a sense of foreboding to the journey, almost as though we're leaving the day behind and heading into the lonely darkness, occupied by events I can't foresee. These are coming, but at least I know they are coming, so making it bearable for a Buddhist cat such as myself – living in the present and taking events as they come is all I can do.

"Freddie cat," says Famke, "we're on the outskirts of a city called Amersfoort. The car two cars behind us is a police vehicle, different from the last time I told you. They're swapping cars really well. Wherever we go, they're going to be right behind us."

"Oh good," I say, "if we go into a walled compound, do we go in or do we get out before we go inside?"

"Good question," says Famke, "I get out and you go

inside. You are a brave cat and incredibly self-sufficient. Are you alright with that?"

"Yes, Famke, I can go inside. I should be okay as long as my collar is intact and the locator is working. We'll find out what happens. I'm probably getting ahead of myself."

"It's good to think about things," replies Famke, "and work out what you might need to do, because you might not have long to think when the situation presents itself. That's what we're told in training Freddie, but you worked it out for yourself... Oh, we're stopping... what's happening?"

"Is it for petrol?" I ask.

"It doesn't look like it. We're on the side of the road. I'll take a look. I'll just hop down to the ground."

Famke flaps silently to the ground and hops a few yards, before taking off and landing on the branch of a tree. I try to listen hard to determine whether someone gets out of the car, as I might need to vacate the premises quickly to avoid being spotted. Famke looks around and watches the lights of a car come in the other direction before disappearing around the corner. Suddenly, another crow joins Famke on the branch. They're in profile and seem animated. Then they both disappear from the branch and Henk appears on the tyre, gliding in for an expert landing on the hub of the wheel.

"Freddie cat," says Henk, "the fearless English cat. Famke is ahead of us and will squawk loudly if the driver appears to be about to drive off. The girl is the daughter of a wealthy business owner, and we think the driver and his accomplice are waiting for another car to come along and transfer her.

The humans will allow this to happen as they want to pick up the entire gang… here's Famke."

"…the driver is on the phone," says Famke, "we might be moving, perhaps a change of plan. I'll fly back…"

For a few seconds, Henk and I wait to see what happens.

"What's this?" says Henk, as a vehicle screeches to a halt on the other side of the road. It is a pickup truck and appears to be white or cream. The two men in my vehicle get out and extricate the girl from the back. I jump down and scoot around to the front of the vehicle. Henk flies off to join Famke. I peer out from behind the roadside front wheel of my SUV. The driver of the pickup opens the back roadside door, and the driver of the SUV deposits the girl in the back. The accomplice from the SUV sits back in the front of his vehicle. All of a sudden, the SUV driver is lying face down in the road. I hear nothing. The driver of the pickup runs across to the passenger side of the SUV and shoots the accomplice. I am in shock, but I remember my road-crossing protocol and scamper across the road while he's on the passenger side of the SUV. Then he drags the man in the road across to the SUV and throws him into the backseat. Whilst he's doing that, I place myself in the back of his truck behind what appears to be a pump, and I make myself small.

My heart is beating out of my chest, and I wish my mum was here, as I am fearful. I try to imagine what she would have said, as the driver executes a U-turn and puts his foot down on the accelerator. She would have said that I should do my best, and so I do my best to calm down. The bad news is that the truck smells of dog, but the good news is that the dog isn't here. You have to find the wheat amongst the chaff sometimes. The driver is being a bit reckless in his driving and cars coming the other way have to move over to avoid a collision, judging by their reactions from my view in the back of the truck. The driver believes he is late, so what could we be late for? Surely not a meeting at a house? Perhaps a plane, a boat, or a train? It must be transportation. It's dark now and I have no idea where I am, of course, as I don't have a local crow for company. We approach a junction with some lighting and there is a crow on a gantry, almost as though I'd wished the bird into existence. The man slows before turning and the crow caws twice, though I can only observe the motion. A vehicle slips out of a side road and comes in our direction, though keeping a long distance away from us. We must be heading for a boat, but not a public boat, as you can't just arrive on a ferry with another human draped over a shoulder like so much excess baggage. People would ask questions, especially if you are waving a gun around.

We slow down a little as though the driver is perhaps concerned at not missing a turning. The darkness is back and even with my eyesight I can't discern much. I hope my locator is working as I look out over the landscape. I can perceive what appears to be a lake and we're not that far from it. The car behind is getting closer. The driver of the truck pulls over to the side of the road and gets out, holding a pair of binoculars. He scans the horizon, and I presume he's looking for a boat. Then I see a light on the lake, and it flickers on and off three times. The man holds his phone up and appears to have a torch app as it lights up the air. This must be it. The rendezvous is at hand. The people in the car which stopped one hundred yards behind would also have seen the signals and will probably call in reinforcements on the landward side as vessels on the water would easily be seen.

The driver gets in the truck and heads towards the lake before making a turn. He turns his lights off and comes to a stop. He gets out again and leans on the bonnet of the truck, looking at the lake through his binoculars. This is not good as the turning is not obvious. The Freddie cat has to do something. I scan the surroundings and discover a small branch in the grass. I see the driver is looking away from me. With stealth, I leap out of the truck and check both ways before crossing the road and grabbing the branch with my mouth.

The branch doesn't taste nice, but it is nice and straight, and I lay it across the road. I get two small twigs or sticks and make an arrow shape, pointing at the turning. I hope this is enough of a clue as it not only shows where the vehicle has gone but also indicates the truck didn't go straight ahead as otherwise the branch would not be located where it is, as the truck would have run over it. I have done my best and I feel sure my mum would appreciate my efforts. I wait on the road as I don't wish to return to the dog kennel on wheels any sooner than I have to.

After two minutes of heart-thumping anticipation, the boat seems to dock, and the man returns to his driving seat and off we go. I sit on the back bumper of the truck as it's wide enough and I don't wish to be seen leaping into the vehicle. I watch the turning of the road from my vantage point and see a car speed past, presumably scattering my carefully prepared arrow. This is not good news, but then a human figure appears at the turning and starts running down the track. Soon there are two others and they're heading my way, too. This is better news and my heart calms a little. But then I hear a dog barking. This is getting exhausting. I jump down from the truck and sit on a small grass mound. I have to keep my wits about me, as I can now be seen and probably smelled by the dog. And then I discern something. There's an inflatable zipping over the waves right by the waterline. It's in the shadows and silently heading towards the docked boat. The driver of the truck gets the girl out of the back and manhandles her towards the boat. Two humans loom out of the dark and take her. She is now struggling hard, and the men's attention is taken up by the writhing of her body. Men from the inflatable are on dry land now and running hard, carrying guns by the looks of it. They keep to the shadows with great success.

Many things happen at once. The truck driver is illuminated in a bright light and a loudhailer gives some instructions I don't understand. The man goes for his gun with his right hand, but his right shoulder almost dissolves from the impact of a bullet and he writhes on the ground. There is a lot of blood and he's crying out in pain. The two men who were holding the hostage are now both unconscious on the ground and the kidnapped girl is being carried towards me by a human, presumably a good guy, as they say in American TV shows.

Some car lights illuminate the scene and a familiar voice says: "Freddie, Freddie, are you here, are you alright?"

I am then illuminated by another torch and turn towards Miep. I miaow to indicate I am fine, but I really do have to have a poo as my body is in a bit of shock, so I move out of the spotlight for a bit of privacy. The torch follows me, but when they see what I'm about to do, the torch is moved away and is replaced by some laughter. Having a poo is a natural thing to do after some excitement as the body is working overtime. Once I am finished, I return to the spotlight, feeling much relieved in at least one way.

I watch as more vehicles come down to where we're located. The girl is placed in a helicopter that lands in the field and is soon whisked off. The wounded man is given some emergency treatment and placed in an ambulance that rushes off, all sirens blazing. Two armed police go with him as he's a dangerous individual. Miep watches impassively at all the activity. She is approached by a man who I believe has come from the inflatable boat. He salutes Miep and then asks her a question. Miep indicates a larger van, and the man turns to his team, who drag the two men from the boat on the water into the back of it, making sure they are handcuffed and have their ankles cuffed together too, so they won't be able to walk well. Three more police get in the back of that van, and it does a neat turn and heads away. Another team has brought some arc-lights that now illuminate the docked boat. Some armed police proceed gingerly on board and make sure there's no one else on board. A dog is chained to one of the rails of the boat and is prancing around on deck like dogs do when they get excited and are unable to control their emotions. Its growls maintain the air of malice at this scene.

Miep looks at me: "None of this would have happened without you, Freddie cat, the rescue of the daughter of an industrialist, the arrest of kidnappers, and the apprehension of a double murderer. In your country, I think if you were a human, you'd get an award for this, yes?"

I miaow – I think she means a George Cross, but I don't believe cats are eligible for this as we don't really have a place to pin the medal. There was the Dickin Medal in WWII awarded to dogs and pigeons mainly and was hung around their necks, but I believe that is no longer awarded in the UK.

Miep's phone goes, and she answers quickly, saying a few short sentences that sound positive. She then looks at me and says in English: "Yes, he's here, he's fine, though I think he's probably hungry and thirsty. Is that right, Freddie?" I miaow, Miep is right. I am hungry and thirsty and could do with a nice restful snooze and the company of a relaxing book for an hour or so. Miep puts her phone away.

"Come on, Freddie, let's get you back to Amsterdam. Gemma followed the man, who tried to steal a picture as a diversion and then smashed a window to escape. Gemma ran after him, and he was very surprised to be arrested a mile away. He forgot that cats can run faster than humans. It's just that most of the time, cats aren't motivated to do so. Gemma jumped on the man's head and scratched him when our officers were close by, just to make sure we arrested the right man."

That does sound like the sort of thing Gemma would do

when she's in spy mode and determined to make sure the criminals don't get away. What Miep says about cats and running is all true, of course, as I'm sure you know by now.

When we get to the turning, I miaow profusely.

"What's the matter?" asks Miep.

I indicate the interior handle of the door and Miep allows me out. I hunt around and find the small branch about five yards down the road. I drag it over to Miep.

"You put that on the road?" asks Miep.

I miaow and place it in the place where I placed it before.

"You think of everything," says Miep, "our car ran over that and then we realised the truck couldn't have gone straight on, so we reversed and saw the boat. You are a very clever cat and strong too, to carry a branch around."

I purr and then move the branch aside as I had made my point, which is all you can ever do, isn't it?

The journey back to Amsterdam is a lot better than the outward journey. I am inside the vehicle for a start and that makes so much difference, especially in terms of warmth. As might be expected, I drift off to sleep and have a dream about staring at a waterfall as the river thunders over the edge of a precipice but is stilled in the large pool below. The water swirls around and around and calms itself, before trickling off in various small streams, continuing its journey to wherever it's going at a steadier and more leisurely pace.

The next thing I know, I'm being carried out of the vehicle into Miep's garden. Through bleary eyes, I recognise a few familiar shapes. I am placed on a soft cushion on a chair and have to have a long stretch as I feel as though I will seize up otherwise. I blink and then recognise Mary, John, Mrs Elkins, Miep, Henk, Famke, and Gemma. This is quite a welcome. The humans rub my fur and stroke me.

Mary gives me quite a worried look. John smiles, Mrs Elkins looks at me as though I am a lucky cat, and Gemma nods to me. Miep says the humans should go inside for a few minutes as they should prepare some food for the animals who've been busy.

This is the debriefing session with Henk. I tell him what had happened after I left him and Famke when the girl was transferred between the two vehicles and the men were shot. Gemma winces when I say this part but pats me on the head when I describe how I made the arrow to indicate where the truck had gone on the remote road.

Henk thanks me and Gemma for all our efforts and says that all the gang are captured, though the two men in the SUV are dead as they have died from their gunshot wounds. The kidnapped girl is under sedation in the hospital and has a guard in case another attempt is made to steal her from her family. The human police are wondering how to convey the story to the newspapers, television stations, and online news outlets, as cats aren't supposed to get involved in police work, however we were seen by various people in cars and the man Gemma followed has the scratches to prove at least one cat was involved. Henk is sure the humans will produce a story and that the press will not want to interview us. He's not sure about the operation on the ship earlier in the day though, as the members of the crew have already told their lawyers that some cats were on board their ship and these cats were not part of the crew. He's almost completely sure that no one took photos of us at any time on the ship.

Finally, Henk says our humans don't know about our escapades on the ship at Europoort but have seen our photos from the protest near the Euromast. Mary and John do know that I was involved in the tailing of the kidnappers, as apparently they saw me in The Rijksmuseum chasing after the man who initially kidnapped the girl. I was the only cat in the vicinity and have a distinctive colour pattern, apparently, so this could not be denied. They didn't see Gemma jumping through a broken window and sprinting after a man at full speed.

The humans come back at this point and bring with them some quite delicious food including some kibbles and a selection of muffins, as someone has noticed that the Freddie cat and the Gemma cat appreciate muffins, especially the chewier ones with a harder texture that are more suited to the function of our teeth. For once, I'm not too concerned about my figure, as I feel as though I will have burned off lots of calories today, mostly from nervous energy. There is also some Edam and Gouda cheese, and we manage to consume a moderate amount of that, as we are both hungry. We're also given a large bowl of water and drink copiously, as this is the first proper drink we've had in about seven hours.

Chapter 13

Today

NEITHER GEMMA NOR I REMEMBER coming into our room last night, so we must have fallen asleep outside and been brought inside and placed in our beds. Whoever did this is kind and also strong as a sleeping cat is not an easy object to carry without waking it up. I had no dreams I could remember. I am quite energised and eat my kibbles with gusto, although it does make me slightly sad this is our last full day in Amsterdam. Anyhow, I must not worry about that and enjoy my time in the city today.

"Were you there when those poor men were shot?" asks Gemma after completing her breakfast routine.

"I was," I reply, "although I didn't hear or witness anything. I reckon the murderer used a silencer on his revolver and I was hiding near the front wheel, so he didn't notice me. I scampered over to his vehicle while he was preoccupied and jumped in the back and hid near a pump."

"Did you look both ways before crossing the road?"

"I did, yes I wouldn't have been much use to anyone if I'd been run over by a car or a bus and squashed."

"That's true, and it's good you had the presence of mind to

remember your road crossing routine in a time of such anxiety."

"I was trying to be calm while not being at all calm. What about your escapade? How did you end up leaping on the man's head?"

"Well," says Gemma, wrapping her tail around her front paws, "I followed the man, as you are aware. I kept to the shadows wherever possible and tried to make sure he wouldn't see me if he did turn around, which mercifully he didn't, otherwise I would have been spotted. Unless he reasoned that cats go around the gallery looking at the paintings, of course…"

"…it's always a possibility, isn't it?" I say, "family pets might get in free after 6pm on Saturdays…you never know…"

"…indeed," says Gemma, readjusting her feet slightly, "but he carried on, disappeared round a corner and made a lunge for a painting as soon as he did so, setting off the alarms of course and then taking his jacket off and wrapping it around his arm, before smashing a window with his arm and jumping through the window, sustaining some snagged clothing in the process. I assessed the situation and saw him running off. I gave chase, but he ran for quite a long way, well away from the museum. Some officers were coming after us, but he turned a corner and then stopped running, discarded his jacket, and pretended to be strolling along. I spotted the officers and then realised I had to attract their attention, so I jumped on the man's head, from behind, of course, and set about him, biting his ear, and scratching his face. He didn't appreciate this, of course, and tried to fend me off, but his arm waving was seen by the officers, and they came to investigate. One of the officers was wearing an earpiece and seemed to receive a message. She placed the man under arrest immediately. The other officer said to me, in English: "You can stop biting him now Gemma, we've got him." I bit his ear one last time and jumped off him. He didn't taste nice. He had eau-de-Cologne on."

Gemma curls her upper lip slightly.

"You did well to bring him to the police's attention."

"Yes, then Arne turned up and said Henk was following you and that they'd caught the other man from the museum, the one who was serving the sandwiches, and grabbed the girl initially. We headed back to the museum where there were a lot of flashing lights and people milling about looking perturbed. Miep had gone already as they were following you, so I waited with Arne, Mary, and John. Our human parents were wondering where you'd gone. They saw you running after someone, but you disappeared. And now we know why."

"Do Mary and John understand why?"

"I'm not sure, I'm not sure. Perhaps we should head into the garden and discover from the conversation."

"That's a good idea, Gemma. I hope there are some muffins left, as I am still hungry. Yesterday took a lot out of me in terms of nervous energy."

"Yes, I'm not surprised to hear you say that," says Gemma as she trots away towards the cat flap and the outside world.

We emerge into a lovely morning. Mary puts down a plate with half a muffin on it for me and Gemma receives a similar offering from John. They also pour water into two saucers and place those on the ground. I wonder if we'll get the same treatment when we go home, perhaps at weekends, when the humans don't have to go to work? I tell myself off as I should concentrate on eating this meal now and not try to foresee what might happen in the future in terms of breakfasts.

There are some old-fashioned items called newspapers on the table and I'm wondering whether we get a mention at all for anything. Again, I tell myself off as I should enjoy the moment when I'm chewing my muffin, which seems to have currants in it and a raspberry or two. It's the correct texture too for a cat's teeth. I decide to chew a piece of muffin, have a slurp of water, and then chew some more muffin. This works really well, and I am content when I've finished. Gemma makes deliberate eye contact with me and then looks at the table. There seems to be a picture in the newspaper. Mary sees me looking:

"Freddie, you and Gemma are in the newspaper."

She shows me the picture and thankfully it's from the protest at the Euromast where Gemma and I are behind a small placard.

I miaow with a little relief as that picture is fine and acceptable as everyone knows that Gemma and I attended that protest.

Miep arrives and waves at Gemma and me. I stare at her and when I attract her attention, I glance at the newspaper and miaow before looking at her again.

Miep picks up the newspaper and reads out that the two English cats, Gemma, and Freddie, attended a protest at the Euromast, and everyone was excited they were there.

Gemma and I exchange an encouraging glance at each other.

"There is another report in this newspaper," says Miep, showing us the newspaper, "where there is some late news about an attempted kidnapping at the Rijksmuseum, of the daughter of an industrialist, which was thwarted by armed police late at night in the countryside to the north of the city. An unusual aspect of the initial kidnapping around the museum was that some people witnessed two cats running after the kidnappers in different parts of the museum. These criminals were apprehended, but the cats disappeared."

Mary smiles at me and John points at Gemma, who tries to appear innocent. Thankfully, there are no pictures in the newspaper of us scampering around inside, but these days you can never quite be sure what will appear on social media when every human's mobile phone has a camera. I now have one of those moments when you suddenly remember something that happened when you were in the middle of being busy doing something else and only spot out of the corner of your eye.

When Famke and I were riding along on the tyre on the back of the SUV and the people in the car behind were looking at us, I now seem to remember seeing someone pointing their mobile phone screen at us. It would just be the sort of thing some people would do, so either they were taking a picture or a video. I was mostly inside the tyre with just my head sticking out, so I hope I couldn't be identified as Freddie the cat.

At this moment, Henk, Famke, and Arne arrive and flutter

over to where Gemma and I are lying down. The humans are finishing off their breakfast and reading either the newspaper or a book. This is nice and relaxing.

"Good morning, English cats," says Henk, "how are you?"

"Morning, Henk," we say, "morning Arne and Famke."

Arne and Famke flap their wings in unison, as is the way with Europol crows. Their coordination is quite remarkable.

"So, some updates," says Henk. "Jan has had his wing set and will be back with us in two weeks. He sends his regards and congratulations on your achievements yesterday. He would have particularly liked to have seen Gemma biting the man in the head, as he reckons that would be worth seeing."

Gemma smirks and waves her paw at Henk, "Tell Jan, from me, that the man tasted of eau de Cologne and he had a horrible, sickly-sweet tang, so I don't advise biting male humans ever."

Famke nods her agreement: "Yes, I pecked a criminal behind the ear once and it was like you say. Horrible. I buried my beak in soil for five minutes to get rid of the flavour."

"That man was arrested and has been charged with three offences," continues Henk, "so he's going to be kept in prison until his trial. The same with the man who carried off the girl and handed her over to the two men in the SUV, the two who were later killed. This girl has said that she thought she saw a cat on a couple of occasions, once at the museum and once in the back of the pickup truck. She says it had whiskers and green eyes, but gave no further identification, so that should be fine, although her father might press us on this issue as we don't officially employ cats on rescue missions."

"Dutch cats have more sense than us," says Gemma, looking at me.

"There are two things that aren't so good," says Henk, "one of the crew of the ship took a picture of you two on the ship, to show his friends, as he wanted to make sure that you weren't the ship's cats and he'd just never seen you before. I'm not sure if this photo was sent anywhere, so we'll try to remove it from his phone, but some people in the defence might say this is tampering with evidence, so we have to be careful. The other is that someone took a picture of you, Freddie cat, and Famke on the back of the SUV and shared it with their friends and it has become quite popular. However, all you can spot is your eyes and ears, so that should be okay. The problem is that the image shows the licence plate and people now know those two men driving that vehicle were later killed, so prosecutors might wonder why a crow and a cat were on the back of the vehicle, was the vehicle under surveillance, that sort of thing."

"You mean that if the girl talks about the cat at the museum and in the pickup truck and this image of the SUV that the girl was in also shows a cat then the defence people will say that the cat was involved throughout the whole surveillance process and how did the cat know where to go and what to do?" asks Gemma.

"Yes, that's more or less it. Who does the cat work for? They won't be able to identify the cat as Freddie, of course, but it's something to bear in mind."

"Well, that's interesting, isn't it?" I say. "I wonder whether the police could be forced to identify me?"

"They might be asked, but they wouldn't say, because it would be against the interests of national security," says Famke.

"I suppose that's some reassurance," says Gemma, "I was half expecting someone to take a picture of me biting the man last night, but he'd chosen a quiet place to stop and throw away his jacket, so that worked in my favour."

Henk nods in agreement.

"Will they be able to identify Famke?" I ask.

"No," says Henk, "to humans most crows are the same, in fact to most humans most rooks and ravens are also crows, as they can't discern the differences, so Famke will be fine, but thank you for asking."

"Thank you, Freddie cat, I'll be fine," says Famke, nodding her head, "it's all in a day's work."

I am a little embarrassed and stare at a tree for ten seconds to get over the slight colouration of my skin under the fur. I can feel it even though no one can see it.

Henk continues: "I hope you enjoy your visit this afternoon and that no one tries to steal anything while you're there, as you might like to tour around a tourist attraction without chasing any criminals."

"Where is it we're going?" asks Gemma.

"It's fairly close," says Famke, "so we can accompany you there, just to make sure that nothing happens."

A nut hits me on the backside, indicating that the two squirrels have arrived, although I can't locate Bertie and Johann anywhere. Their camouflaging skills are excellent.

"They're hiding in the tree behind you," says Gemma, "on

the fourth branch up from the ground on the right-hand side, about a third of the way along. They've been there for two minutes."

Gemma is back in spy mode again and ducks out of the way of a nut thrown at her with a nonchalant movement of her head.

"Squirrels don't wear eau-de-Cologne, do they?" she says, looking with distaste at the rodents in the tree.

Henk gives a squawk and a crow lands on the branch by the two squirrels and appears to impart some information to them whereupon no further nuts head our way. Put it like this, if looks could kill, then Johann wouldn't be feeling very well right now.

Mary and John head over to us and give us a stroke, which I enjoy, and Gemma endures as she's still looking towards Johann with some anger. Gemma is improving at her anger management, but still needs to be calmer in certain situations.

"We're going for a walk, Gemma and Freddie, and you should come too. They've laid on a surprise visit for you and it's not far, so let's go kitties," says Mary.

Gemma has a quick wash, which is her preferred method of counting to ten when she's trying to come to terms with something. I dawdle until she finishes and then we scoot along, trying to get a bit of exercise. I am a bit stiff from my crouching of the previous day and being hunched inside a tyre, so I run around moving my legs in slightly unnatural ways to try to get the muscles stretched. I suppose if I were human, I'd request a massage, but I've never seen any advertisements for cat masseurs, so this has to be a do-it-myself project. Gemma trots along and doesn't seem to be bothered by my meandering around. She is focused on something, but I'm not sure on what.

Miep walks ahead and almost seems to be making sure that no one comes towards us with any bad intentions. I feel better for my moving around and decide it's time to move in a straight line for a change.

"Do you know where we're going?" I ask.

"I reckon so, you have to remember that humans aren't good at being imaginative, so does that give you a clue?"

"We're cats, so they'll want us to be rewarded for our good work yesterday and to go somewhere relaxing and without surprises, so where better than… oh The Cat Cabinet. We're going there."

"Yes, the KattenKabinet would be the best place to go. We were shown it on our previous visit, but we didn't make it, did we? Let's hope no one is trying to rob the place or kidnap the son of an oil sheikh who is keen on cats when we arrive."

"Yes, it would be good just to have a nose around and not have any criminal diversions. You're right, as usual."

We are heading along Herengracht, and I know that Gemma is correct even before we see the place itself.

"Surprise," says John.

I miaow as I'm pleased to be here. Gemma looks a little pityingly at John, but I think she appreciates the thought. I hope that no one comes running out of the KattenKabinet clutching an exhibit they've stolen, and I have to give chase, because I really don't want to convey to the reader that all the museums and galleries have items stolen from them on a daily basis, because they don't.

Cats don't write travel guides or travelogues telling readers where they went and what they saw when they went there. Suffice to say, if you like cats in posters, paintings, and in statue form, this is the place for you. A guide showed us around, and everything is really lovely, though for me what is even more wonderful than the exhibits is how the human visitors are enjoying these items and interacting with them. This is the better side of human nature and gives me hope for the future, a future taken one moment at a time.

www.ingramcontent.com/pod-product-compliance
Lightning Source LLC
LaVergne TN
LVHW091250080426
835510LV00007B/189